aged a code of ethics where the strong protected the weak and you played by the rules.

Once the game gained this form of respectability, it was embraced by the Universities. Each undergraduate brought with him his own variations and you can imagine the howls of protest when a player from one background broke the taboos of another. Committees were set up and the various customs and practices were melded into a common code. However, there was a genuine schism between those who saw the quintessence of the game as catching, kicking and running and those who espoused the virtue of controlling the ball with the feet. Each group kept elements of each other's game, the goalkeeper in soccer being an obvious example, but generally they grew apart. Those who preferred rugby–probably the stronger and more aggressive or those who liked the thrill of the matador–played their game, whilst those who preferred the skills of dribbling–probably the less strong but more nimble–chose the version that was to become soccer. No doubt there were those who still hankered after the basic battle and objected to any restriction on aggression and violence. However, they must have been in a minority and, like the remainder of the marginalised flock, set off to find a new life in America.

It is important to realise that this split between rugby and soccer did not at that time reflect any social division. The toffs had rescued and refined the game that they had so openly despised in the past. In addition, they developed a sophistication of playing skills and a code of sportsmanship that was to influence recreational activities throughout the world. The working class had no such opportunities and it must have seemed at the time that sporting recreation for the masses had all but disappeared. But, again, the gods of irony were at hand.

Although the graduates from the Universities were top-drawer, they could not all inherit the estate or take over the family business. What happened to the football-playing younger sons of younger sons? Many went into the Armed Forces, where any propensity for violence or employment of tactical acumen was amply accommodated. For the others, there were the professions, a return to Education, or the Church.

Many a young curate started his ministry in the impoverished parishes of the industrial cities. He would quickly realise the value of bribery if he were to make any headway with his incipient flock. *Come to Sunday School in the morning and I'll organise a game of football in the afternoon.* From such acorns, the Premiership oak has grown. As the absence of grass or, at least, grass you were allowed to walk on, was a defining feature of inner city life, all ball games had to be played on a relatively enclosed hard surface. The dribbling game was the obvious choice. Unlike rugby, there were no confusing rules to undermine instinctive effort. No steep learning curve to be acquired before you were permitted to take part, and serious injury was kept to a minimum.

Once the various Factory Acts allowed the working man to have Saturday afternoon off and the Football Association set up the FA Cup, which necessitated a consistent set of national rules, soccer broke away from its upper class roots and was embraced by the masses who played it in youth and watched it with equal fervour when the flesh became less willing. So, for the most part, the version espoused by former pupils of Rugby School was played only by the élite.

And the schism was reinforced by those who went into teaching and had a somewhat different agenda. Many would return to their Alma Mater, or somewhere reassuringly similar. They knew that the game had a greater purpose than saving souls or preaching that cleanliness was next to godliness. There was an Empire to serve and the new social stratifications to maintain. You played not for the glory of yourself but for the glory of your House, your School and your Queen and Country. Rugby football, with its sense of internal discipline and bravery in the face of adversity, filled the bill. Henry Newbolt's 'Vitaï Lampada' said it all. Although the illustrative sport is cricket, the principle is the same.

There's a breathless hush in the Close to-night
Ten to make and the match to win—
A bumping pitch and a blinding light,
An hour to play and the last man in.
And it's not for the sake of a ribboned coat,
Or the selfish hope of a season's fame,
But his Captain's hand on his shoulder smote—
Play up! Play up! and play the game!

By the second stanza, the 'last man in' finds himself as a junior officer in the desert with 'the gatling jammed and the colonel dead', having to face the swarming hordes of oncoming tribesmen. Of course, his pubescent experience saw him through.

But there was also a practicality in the choice. Whereas soccer deliberately reduced the number of players to allow the greater opportunity for skill and individualism and to encourage the passing game introduced by itinerant Scottish mercenaries, the public schoolmaster saw the need to involve as many people as possible. After all, the pupils had to be occupied during the whole of their waking hours. Individualism was not stifled but compartmentalised. In rugby, each would have a share of the glory but none the sole claim. The dashing winger who scores the try knows—and knows others know—that he would never have done so without the initial possession from scrum or maul. The kicker of the vital penalty equally accepts that others have gained the field position that made it possible. The soccer star, on the other hand, could start on his own goal line and dribble the length of the field to score without having to rely on any assistance from his team-mates—and often did.

So the game of rugby evolved to fit the range of players available. The powerful non-ball players could be props playing a game where they were rarely called upon to touch the ball with the hand; the tall could leap in the lineout and use their long levers to impart power to the scrum; the eager and partially competent were scavenging wing forwards. The small, with the advantage of a low centre of gravity, were scrum halves if they could kick and pass, and hookers if they couldn't. In the backs, the general and most skilful ball player was pivotally located at fly half, the best tacklers in the centre, the quick who could leave you for dead on the wing and, at full back, the nearest the school had to the imperturbable Crab Jones. This also made a virtue out of necessity as many schools had relatively few pupils and it was very unlikely that chance would produce fifteen all-round athletes in one academic year. Each learned his role and the school/ringmaster ran the show.

As for the Americans, they embraced the violent version, reduced it to eleven-a-side and took to charging at each other whilst taking it in turns to guard the ball. Propulsion by neither foot nor hand was allowed. Death was not unusual, particularly as a result of the Flying Wedge. Five of the burliest would link arms in a V formation protecting the ball carrier and with a concerted effort try to trample a path through the perceived weakest member of the opposition. Too often, neither side succeeded in scoring. This was, of course, completely against the American idea of a proper result. So they changed the rules to cash in on the quickness of eye and fleetness of foot they had observed in their recently-released servant classes.

2

And Who Did *Your* Father Play For?

In circa 5BP * Jason Leonard moved from Saracens to Harlequins. The new boy was welcomed by a member of that particular establishment with an enquiry as to which school he had attended. Leonard replied, 'Warren School'. As this was not immediately recognised, his interlocutor was compelled to rifle through his well-tuned cerebral index of minor public schools in the south of England. Leonard, sensing a problem, added helpfully, 'It's a comp. in Chadwell Heath.'

The story illustrates two points. First, Leonard had to move clubs to ensure his international career and, second, even at the dog-end of the 20th century, in certain rugby circles social background was as im-

---

* *Before Professionalism. It is very difficult to pinpoint the exact moment of the annunciation. Some would argue that it was at the point when the game collided with the front pages of the tabloids. Others, the formation of Super 12 Rugby. And there again, the group who in 1895 gathered at the George Hotel in Huddersfield might have its own view on the subject.*

portant as playing ability. This carefully nurtured state of affairs had existed from time immemorial and, as a result, had had a considerable effect on the development (or lack of) of the game in England. The structure of the 'rugger' club reflected much more the social mores of a particular group than a design to promote the game *per se*. The result of this structure was a ramshackle international side that consistently underperformed. The rugby club was like any other masonic activity—the more exclusive it was, the more it excluded.

The whole affair was reminiscent of the time when I was considering the law as a potential occupation. To make even the first hurdle depended on an interview with three wise men from the Law Society. As it turned out, the cross-examination consisted of merely three questions. My answers to the first two, occupation of father and school attended, seemed to pass muster. But I was totally unprepared for the third: 'So, young man, why have you decided to enter the profession?' It was a bit like asking, 'Why did you decide to go to school?' You had to do something and law sounded vaguely reassuring. I remembered I had been quite impressed by Sidney Carton in *A Tale of Two Cities* who seemed able to consume vast amounts of alcohol yet still be more than a match for Mr Justice Mumble-Jumble but instinct warned against this line of approach. So, 'I don't really know,' was the best I could manage. There was a pause whilst the Magi seemed to communicate by telepathy until the most avuncular of the trio smiled, 'Exactly so. We are sure you will be very successful.'

How did this exclusivity come about? After all, the ex-public schoolboys who chose the soccer route felt no need to build such monuments, or even purchase their own grounds. Perhaps we should look at the intrinsic nature of a football club. In its essence it seems to be a convenient way of providing the necessities for the game—a pitch to play on, changing facilities and a ball and goals.

There were two ways this could happen. Either a patron could provide the wherewithal or a group of like-thinkers could combine and share the expense. Mill and factory owners recognised the prestige attached to a successful football team and were willing to fund the operation and, more significantly, give their employees time off to train and play. They also realised the financial advantages of staging popular sporting events. Hence the present-day professional soccer club—a commercial institution funded by the

31

sale of its wares, be they exhibitions of footballing skill or shirts carrying the name and number of the current diva (pronounce as you see fit).

The other route, that of self help, was of course open to either code, but became the preserve of rugby. The most probable reason for this was the need to fund in advance. If a club cost £100 to run, twenty individuals would have to guarantee, at the outset, £5 each. If the club had as official patron a wealthy mill owner, he would pay upfront and re-coup his losses from the 'gate', which only required 100 people paying 5p on twenty occasions. So, the nature of any 'supporter' of the club was determined by the amount he earned. Clearly, the working class had little choice. It supported the game where you paid relatively small amounts when you could, and tried to climb over the fence when you couldn't.

The sporting middle classes could afford to fund themselves and, by doing so, control their destiny. It had its own cachet. If you were a member of such a club, it meant that you could afford to be: it was a way for the parvenu to announce his arrival from obscurity. But this does not answer the question of why they chose rugby. The answer is that, in the eyes of some, soccer had sold itself to the devil. The symbolic moment was when the FA introduced the concept of a penalty kick if a player was deliberately fouled when trying to shoot for goal. The purist footballer argued that no sportsman would do such a thing and therefore the rule was redundant. The FA, which ran a competition that made tens of thousands of pounds, not surprisingly thought otherwise.

Only a naïf would believe that the real world of the 19th century was run on Christian principles. Indeed, the Empire owed its success to exploiting others, both at home and abroad, but for some there was a Never Never land of sport where people behaved properly and with due regard for the rules. In your day-to-day existence you might have to behave badly to make money but for an hour or so you could operate at the virtuous level of playing according to the rules. Some, like schoolmasters, priests and poets, had learnt to avoid the grim reality (though were happy enough to receive the dividends). Others grasped at the straw of rugby and its amateur ethos, feeling that it could, indeed should, be the final bastion in the fight against declining moral and ethical standards.

But the distinction between idealism and élitism soon became blurred. As a one-time president of

Yorkshire remarked on the subject of broken time—if you can't afford to take time off work, you shouldn't play rugby. And it was not long before the middle classes took the game as their own. In fact, the sporting event ceased to be the sole *raison d'être*. For some, it was an opportunity to network, for others a halfway house between student ribaldry and sententious membership of the golf club.

But the outward show was a crusade. A crusade, uniformed in blazers and ties, that set out to protect the virtue of the game and all it stood for. The Infidel was the player who attempted to make a living out of his footballing skills, or those who attempted to pay him. They were to be sought out and excommunicated with all the zeal of the McCarthy witch hunts. To this end, the Rugby Football Union (the choice of union rather than association is interesting in itself) set up a complex interlocking structure. It took as its model one which was familiar to all who were likely to be involved: the public boarding school. The President, aided by his officers, was the headmaster. The Counties and other Constituent Bodies were the prefects who controlled the day-to-day running of the game. The Clubs, in various ranks, were the body of the school, and the players the much put-upon fags. The philosophy of the game was decided by committee. Each club had a representative on the county committee and each county had a representative on the main committee of the Union. In theory, this was a democratic constitution that would allow the youngest member of the least significant club to have his say in the running of affairs. In practice, the opposite happened. Decisions were taken at the top and the apparent democratic process became little more than a chain of command to ensure that the grass roots did as they were told.

As the Rugby Football Union took over the running of the game, it must, necessarily, be held responsible for the outcome of its actions. The structure and ethos it had invented to safeguard its interests seemed to stultify rather than develop the game and the national team consistently underperformed as a result. Even a half-interested observer could have seen that, if you wanted a successful England side, you must put the players at the centre rather than on the periphery of the action, and that a number of sensible innovations that were eventually swept in on the wave of professionalism could have been implemented decades before. So why was nothing done? Basically, because the people who ran the game, the

Committee Men, were not prepared to rock the boat. As with all institutions of this type, there were offices to be held that accorded distinction and privilege. It was in everyone's interests to toe the line. Also, the successful committee man was of a particular type. He needed to be able to devote considerable portions of his free time to carrying out the job, be sufficiently well off to cover the incidental expenses and, most importantly, be intuitively in tune with the underlying ethos of the game. This combination produced a limited, if not reactionary, response to any idea of change. Or, to put it another way, you don't see many young, female, West Indian bus drivers in the Committee Box at Twickenham.

Until the recent introduction of leagues, the Fixture List also stultified the game. This was another concept taken from school to club. The fixture list was the hairspring that ran public school rugby. First, the opposition had to be of the right class and, second, all sides involved must have a reasonable chance of winning. It was expected that from time to time one school would have an exceptional year and perhaps go unbeaten but in the great scheme of things every dog had its day. It was a sensible scheme for schools as there is little point in the developing player being involved in matches which are won or lost by 50 points. When a similar system was adopted by the clubs, it had rather a different effect. Each club wanted to enhance its tradition and reputation and used the fixture list to achieve this. A skilful Fixture Secretary could build a list that increased the club's status. As a result, the better players were attracted to the club, which improved the results, which acted as a lever to climb further up the ladder. All matches were 'friendlies' and you played by invitation only. The skill in balancing the fixture list books in your favour was to persuade those above to send you an invitation while ridding yourself of the dross below. In the end, it became a matter of influence rather than a reflection of merit. Players were torn between loyalty to their existing club and a desire to play at a higher standard. Too often, this dilemma halted a player's development and when he finally reached his proper level he found he was at the end of his career. The introduction of leagues, though it had its downside, changed this and gave the game a momentum it had previously lacked. It soon became clear that some of the so-called Senior Clubs had only retained their status by avoiding contact with the competition. The fixture list now reflected playing merit rather than partiality. Players knew where they stood. Clubs could plan ahead. They could become part of the community as a whole rather than an élite inner circle.

If the RFU had been just another Gentlemen's Club basking in 19th-century obsolescence, it would have been of little consequence. But it wasn't. It controlled a game that should have expanded its scope and ambition along with the rest of society. By 1970, people wanted the national team to represent the rugby public of England at large and not just a coterie of well-heeled clubs in the Home Counties. Free entry into the grammar schools meant that people from all walks of life were being introduced to the game, where the standard of coaching and organisation was extremely high. But when a player left school, he stepped back a couple of decades and easily became disillusioned. There was no structure for identifying talent and the route to representative honours came through the senior clubs. Even this pool was limited to those players who had the opportunity to take time off work to train and play. Each club became its own empire, jealously guarding its playing assets while eyeing up the assets of others. The RFU was aware of this but did nothing to help. Indeed, the cult of individualism was to be discouraged, not rewarded. The Union seemed happy that matters remained in this stultified state as it suited some greater purpose. It took Will Carling's inadvertent reference to antiquated flatulence to bring matters to a head. The RFU acted with unaccustomed alacrity. Carling, like some impudent Fourth Former, was hauled before the beak, had his wrist slapped and was stripped of the England captaincy. That, they thought, was that.

But it wasn't. The England players refused to accept the decision. They knew that they had achieved success despite rather than because of the RFU. It was common knowledge that some members of the Committee thought the players were getting too big for their boots. Suddenly the emperor's clothes were seen for what they were. First, that there should be such an over-reaction to such a relatively inoffensive remark showed an inflated sense of self-importance. Second, that their control of the playing side of the game was illusory. It had, for practical purposes, gone professional. Demand for tickets far outstripped supply. The top players were generating millions of pounds. The tabloids had started to report the game. Rugby magazines were at the front of the newsagent's stall instead of skulking between *Model Railways* and

Health and Efficiency. The players were going to be paid and if the RFU didn't pay them, then some colonial entrepreneur most certainly would. So, with indecent haste, the game was declared open. Of course, there was no apparatus in place to deal with the outcome of this decision. As a result there was chaos. TV moguls pounced. Individuals with no real allegiance to the game stepped in, waving chequebooks. Boatloads from South Africa, Australia, New Zealand and a raft of South Sea Islanders arrived to hawk their talents to the highest bidder. The result was that clubs, both large and small, put themselves in financial difficulties and, more ominously, the game began to move from being a participant to a spectator sport. In short, all that Rugby Union had stood for was under threat. Saladin was no longer at the door but in the house, not through superior tactics or worth, but because someone had gone out for a pint and left the back gate unlocked. If those responsible were to comply with the tradition they had so long espoused, then the time had come to open the drawer and take out the revolver.

It was not as though they had no warning. Both Association Football and cricket had shown that players who create wealth eventually want a share of it.

There was also evidence to show that the confusion caused by trying to bolt 19th-century values on to a 21st-century way of thinking is easily exploited by those who are less susceptible to the scruples of amateurism. Perhaps the apparent success of a century earlier had given rise to a sense of over-confidence. Rugby Union felt that, once the dust had settled, the professional game of rugby had been confined to a narrow strip of land in the north of England while the rest of Britain was more or less unblemished. It was true there had been the odd spectacular defection but for the most part this was Welsh and, for all they knew, working class anyway. In their self-congratulation, the RFU conveniently overlooked the fact that, before the split, many of the best English rugby players had come from the north and that, to a greater or lesser extent, it was fielding a Second XV. And this 'success' was in a different age. Travel and free time were limited. It suited the supporters of Rugby League to have the games played in a close locality. A Roses clash provided enough week-to-week interest. The cream on the cake was an annual visit to Wembley and the much-awaited visits of the Australians. League enthusiasts claimed, with some justification, that they had the better game in every respect and there was no need to envy or fear the alternative code. The supporters of Union had, as I have suggested, a rather different view of the game and national ambition. The fact that England rarely fulfilled its potential might be lamentable but should not spoil a good supper. The general contribution to the cause was the chorus of *Oh, come on, England!* uttered in the this-hurts-me-more-than-it-hurts-you tone of the long-suffering schoolmaster. Little thought was given as to why they didn't come on.

It was easy to make money the dividing line between perceived good and evil. Those who needed money if they were to be able to play, played League. Those who didn't were by definition welcomed into the Union fold. Both sides had what they needed to hold the moral high ground. Even the RFU would have found it hard to exclude players on the grounds of flat hats and even flatter vowels. But times change. As all sport grew more competitive, so the various demands on players grew proportionately. Eventually, top Union players had to be rewarded. Sometimes it was merely cash under the table, on other occasions reward in kind. The simplest form of this was the player being offered a not-too-demanding job with working hours that were sufficiently flexible to accommodate his playing needs. The beauty of this particular piece of legerdemain was that it rewarded the player for playing without really paying him to do so. In the end it exploited the distinction between a salary and a paid wage at an hourly rate. By such means the RFU, like the rest of the Establishment, was able to assimilate the working class talent identified by the grammar school system. I recall a conversation between two rugby players, each prominent in his own code, discussing relative financial remuneration. The discussion ended with the Union's player's comment, 'Well, Joe, the only difference I can see is that you pay tax on yours.'

Meanwhile, the game prospered. Clubs whose ranks were swelled by players who had been introduced to a game they would never otherwise have played started to run five or six teams. Demand for International tickets increased. The 1991 World Cup had brought the game to a new audience who saw it as something at which their country might excel. If, at this time, the Union had done a sensible audit, it could have remained in control of the game. However it did not and commercial interests outside the game were given the opportunity to shape its destiny. It was abundantly clear that, as the 20th century entered its final decade, rugby could no longer be considered purely in terms of recreation. Equally, those who participated in making it the entertainment industry and profit-making business that it had become, deserved to be rewarded.

There was a variety of routes that might have accommodated the inevitable change, yet retained the essential elements of the game. For example, one could have been based–in the same way as travelling expenses–on the financial loss the player incurred to fulfil the required commitment. If, in order to play, a player surrendered his job opportunity elsewhere, he should be compensated. In addition, his reward should be commensurate to the value he added to the game. The extremes are clear. An England player should receive a good deal; the doctor who is a member of the Extra Bs nothing at all. The exact point when sport moves beyond recreation is difficult to decide and any decision must be arbitrary. A line would have to be drawn, but not necessarily set in stone, and would be regularly reviewed to reflect the general state of the game.

A solution might have been constructed along these lines. The RFU would identify a group of players who would be centrally contracted and form the national squad. The squad would be prepared and coached by RFU-appointed professionals. The players would be encouraged to play for the club of their choice but the number of games they were allowed to play would be limited. This would allow proper preparation for Internationals and prevent overplaying. Clubs would know when they would lose their stars, probably in equal proportion, and plan accordingly. Centrally-contracted players would receive no payment from their club but would be allowed to earn what money they could from off-field activities.

Clubs would be allowed to pay their non-RFU players but all salaries would be capped. The rate of pay allowed would depend on the status of the club within the league system. A cut-off point would be set, say for argument's sake, at National League Two, and below such a point the playing of the game would remain strictly amateur. In reality, not all players would be paid the same or even paid at all, but the League Clubs would still be the route to full-time employment and therefore be attractive in their own right. Capped salaries are the key. The Antipodean star back is, of course, welcome but should not expect to receive any more than the tight head who is supplying him with the ball.

The only exception to this would be that any club would be allowed to remunerate a sensible coaching structure, such a structure to reflect its status in the game. A Premiership Club would perhaps employ a team of three, a Junior Club a player-coach who could also teach by example. The RFU would support this with a pro-rata grant to every club in the Union. In return, it could insist that clubs, particularly Premiership Clubs, produce development teams to identify and encourage young players. Academies are all very well, but if we concentrate only on the élite, where are the community players to come from? An additional advantage of such a structure is that it would create a career pathway for ex-players.

Apart from this, and the necessary medical care, the game should remain completely amateur. Aside from the bare administrative essentials, the game could be run as it always had been. My impression is that, at the time in question, this is what the majority of players wanted. They did not relish the idea of 7/52 wall-to-wall rugby. I, belatedly, recommend the suggestion on three grounds. It is equitable and even-handed. It allows the player and club to improve their lot through their own efforts. Most important, the game would remain in the hands of those who value it, rather than those who wish to exploit it.

Of course, it could be abused. The star Aussie could be paid an astronomical wage to iron the first team shirts or the Clubs could à la soccer just ignore the Union. But as the RFU, via the sale of International tickets and TV rights, held the purse strings and there was a considerable body of opinion that supported the existing ethos, it might have been worth giving it a go and acting as a possible example of controlled professionalism for Unions throughout the world. Sad to say, this was all realised too late. Once the head was removed from the sand, attempts were made by the RFU to regain control and restructure the game in the light of current thinking. It is to be hoped that eventually the game will return to an even keel but all such attempts have, by force of circumstance, been reactive rather than proactive. To the man or woman on the ground, as famous clubs fold and playing numbers decline, it looks very much a case of rearranging the deck chairs on the Titanic.

3

The Hundred Years War

In King Lear, Shakespeare presents the spectacle of an autocratic, self-indulgent king who, through his stupidity, destroys his kingdom. This main action is entwined by a subplot in which an autocratic, self-indulgent duke similarly destroys his family. The theatrical purpose of the two plots is to build up the suspense by allowing the folly of one to be mirrored in the folly of the other. The audience watches in disbelief. Surely they can't both be so stupid? In the theatre, the action takes a few hours, the reality it purports to represent a few months. In the real life of rugby football, a similar state of affairs continued for the best part of a century.

The curtain of this particular drama officially opened with the formation of the Northern Union in 1895 and the consequent evolution of Rugby League. However, the Prologue had been playing for some time. It is generally assumed that the split between the two codes was simply about being paid to play.

In fact it was more complex than that. No one really minded sportsmen making money out of their skill and reputation. After all, at the time in question W G Grace made £9000 out of his various cricketing testimonials without any suggestion that he should be barred from the portals of the MCC. Nor, as is sometimes suggested, was the pro/am argument simply a North/South divide. There were many officials in the North who went to great lengths to support the amateur ethos, none more so than the Reverend Frank Marshall, Headmaster and Committee Man extraordinary. Even a cursory glance at the events of the time show him to be at the centre of all disputes, drawing up regulations and presiding over inquisitions in an attempt to safeguard the amateur spirit. The underlying problem was twofold: a parochial struggle between powerful factions and class distinction.

Although there were subsets of local rivalry in the other Northern Counties, the clash in Yorkshire between the County Committee and the Yorkshire Clubs illustrates the first problem area. The County Committee had essentially two roles: to act as the local representative for the English Rugby Union in ensuring that the official rules and regulations were carried out, and to organise the County's representative sides and Cup competitions. The Clubs' role was to provide games of rugby for players and spectators alike. To add to the problem, there was a further split between those clubs who regarded themselves as Senior and those who were unwilling to accept the subordinate role that such a distinction implied.

When decisions had to be made, matters were confused because the County Committee was made up of representatives of the individual clubs in the county. Each representative might well have his own set of opinions when wearing one hat which could easily clash with the moment when he was wearing another. Whenever discussion took place, the following hidden agenda was never far from the surface:

ITEM 1. International Representation [The feeling that there were never enough Northern, and particularly Yorkshire, players in the national side.]

ITEM 2. Venue for Future Meetings [As all decisions were made at meetings held in London and usually late in the afternoon, the opinions of the Northern delegates were often not given due consideration.]

ITEM 3. The Amateur Game [If players are to be compensated by being paid for 'broken time', does this make them professional?]

ITEM 4. National Competitions [The nature of inter-club competition: should it be a knock-out cup organised by the County or a series of leagues run by the Clubs themselves?]

ITEM 5. Future Planning [Whether, in the event of leagues being formed, there should be a premier division run by the Senior Clubs.]

ITEM 6. AOB [Will the way I vote affect my chances of being awarded high office?]

There must have been moments that would have taxed the wisdom of Solomon and therefore it is not surprising that the baby ended up being cut in half.

Even matters where Northern members would agree (Items 1 and 2, for example) would add fuel to the general conflagration that was to come. The England XV was chosen after a North v South Trial, the result dominating the subsequent selection. On the odd occasion when the South won, Northern players were omitted, with usually disastrous results and consequent display of Northern delight. What is more, Yorkshire dominated the County Championship and would not miss the opportunity to remind everybody of the fact. To add insult to injury, the power base remained firmly in London, despite requests that the annual meeting should alternate between South and North. There is no doubt that at times a member of the County Committee felt that his allegiance to the parent body was being sorely tested. The issue of representation also spilled over into the debate on broken time. Working-class players found it difficult to take a morning off work, let alone several months, so any touring side consisted solely of those who could afford to go. This, in turn, no doubt created the image of the arrogant English sportsman abroad and the Northern working-class player objected to being tarred by the same brush. There is an interesting foot-note to all this.*

In fact, the paying of players was an issue but not part of the disagreement between County and Club. The matter of compensation for wages lost through playing, or broken time as it was known, was gener-ally approved in the North. It was formally raised by the President of the Yorkshire RU in 1893 as to whether it was right and fair that the working man had to submit to a loss which his salaried counter-

---

A century later, a Labour-controlled local authority in the North of England threatened to sack one of its employees if he took time off to travel on a Rugby Union tour with the British Lions. Revenge, it seems, is a dish best served cold.

parts had not to face. As Trevor Delaney records in his examination of the beginnings of Rugby League, even that great defender of the amateur, Frank Marshall, spoke in favour:

> *How is it possible for a workingman, with a wage from 15 and 25 shillings a week, perhaps with a wife and children to support, to play football unless he is compensated for loss of time? It is manifestly clear that the wages lost on Saturday morning is an appreciable factor in the provision for the week's expenses, and that the man can ill afford to lose the amount, small though it may be in actual cash. There is no getting over this argument.*

What is more, even after the split, Rugby League tried to prevent the game going completely professional. First, by capping the money a player could earn and, when that became impossible to control, by insisting that all players held down a proper job at which they worked at least three days a week. Jobs such as 'billard hall marker' or 'bookies runner' were not deemed proper. There seemed to be no headlong rush into the much-feared working-class idleness incurred through professional sport.

At the heart was the conflict between the Yorkshire Committee who ran the County Cup Competition and the Senior Clubs who wanted to organise their fixtures on a more formal basis. T'owd Tin Pot would draw immense crowds (in 1892, 27,654 watched a third-round tie between Leeds and Halifax, a larger crowd than the FA Cup Final of the previous year) and the Yorkshire Committee was justifiably proud of the fact that its endeavours had made rugby the predominant form of football in the county. It felt the Cup competition was the key to this success and its esteem should not be diluted by the alternative of 'league' matches. There was strong support for this view in the other Northern counties who ran their own Challenge Cup Competitions. Only Cheshire, which was always regarded as part of Surrey by those who lived north of the Mersey, had doubts, believing it tended to promote bad feeling.

The Clubs realised that money was to be made if they were able to invest all fixtures with a similar significance to that of the Cup and the best way to do it was to run a League competition with a resultant champion. The English Rugby Union was totally against this proposal, believing that 'friendly' matches were at the heart of the amateur game. The only way that the Senior clubs could achieve their aim was to present a *fait accompli* and, in due course, the premier clubs of Yorkshire and Lancashire would do just that and famously meet at the George Hotel in Huddersfield to found the Northern Union. It would be run, not by the respective Counties, but by representatives of the clubs in question and its aim would be to sustain a separate League structure in the two counties which would produce a final to decide the Champion of the Union. The English Rugby Union, through their County Committees, would naturally forbid the formation of such a scheme. The Senior clubs in Yorkshire would resign and the play would begin.

So it was parochialism rather than professionalism that lay at the heart of the dispute and, although apparently resolved by the parties going their separate ways, it was never far from the surface. When, as chairman, I had to appoint a team manager for an England Schools' side, I approached a gentleman from Yorkshire to see if he would be interested in taking on the job. He was clearly flattered by the invitation but felt it was necessary to express his reservations. 'Well, Graham, it's a great honour. But I must warn you that when it comes down to it, it'll be Wakefield first, Yorkshire second and the North third. However, if all that can be accommodated, I'd love to take on the job.' I have no doubt that, if he thought I had heard of them, he would have preceded his list with the relevant parish and district.

The second element was simply snobbery. At the end of the 19th century the middle classes were now a multi-layered group suspicious of those above but united in their determination to keep those below at bay. They saw the working man as a potential danger. The rise of Trades Unionism and its attendant strikes appeared to threaten the social order—as Orwell put it, 'a sinister flood that threatened to sweep all culture and decency out of existence'. Already, the working man had taken over the game of Association Football and was now threatening to dominate the handling code. Northern players formed the backbone of the England team. Yorkshire ruled the County Championship. Most of the players concerned were working class. The Southern teams were regularly outclassed but the power base remained firmly in London, where the decisions were made. The simplest way to preserve their noble game was to ban payment in any form, thus reserving the game for those who could afford to play and thus, by definition, belonged to the right social grouping.

The witch hunt was intense, at times almost ri-

diculous. In the days before decimalisation, a player from Northumberland was selected to represent his country at Twickenham. As allowed, he submitted his expenses of £2 to cover the journey from Newcastle to London and back. He received the following note from the Treasurer: 'Third Class rail fare from Newcastle Central to London King's Cross– £1.19s.11d. Cheque herewith.' On the next occasion, he again submitted a similar expense claim but this time with an accompanying note: 'Travel from Newcastle to London–£1.19s.11d. Use of Gentlemen's Lavatory at King's Cross–1d. Total–£2. 0s. 0d.'

Although broken time was frowned upon, it had, as we have seen, some powerful supporters in the amateur ranks. If it had been the sole issue it might have been possible that a solution would have been found, if only by the usual Establishment expedient of turning a blind eye. But there was a greater evil at hand–the payment of inducements in cash or kind to a player to leave one club and join another. Here the English Rugby Union could always find support from those clubs who felt they had lost their stars through under-the-counter deals. Divide and rule was again the order of the day. As in all witch hunts, old scores were settled, traps were set and unsubstantiated accusations abounded. Against all sense of natural justice, a player and club, once accused, had to prove their innocence of any charges made.

Eventually matters had to come to a head and they did—at a General Meeting held in the Westminster Hotel in London in 1893 to discuss the subject of broken time. The representative from North Leeds moved the motion, *That players be allowed compensation for bona fide loss of time.* The proposal was defeated 282-136. The Northern Clubs felt that they had been subject to a conspiracy. First, the Rugby Union had charged their president William Cail to oppose the motion. Cail's views as President would carry weight with the uncommitted. Moreover, he was the representative from Northumberland and suggested, falsely, that other than Yorkshire the Northern Counties were not in favour. The Union had also collected 120 proxy votes from clubs that were known to be against broken time and it was argued that, as many of these came from separate Oxbridge colleges rather than through the Universities themselves, they were invalid. On top of this was the running sore that the meetings were always held in London, making it more difficult for the supporters of the Northern motion to attend. This was the moment when Agenda Item 6 (*vid sup*) came into play: the voting was by a show of hands. On the strength of this victory, the English RU Committee immediately started rewriting the rule book. By-law 1 said it all:

> *The name of the Society shall be the 'Rugby Football Union' and only clubs composed entirely of amateurs shall be eligible for membership and its headquarters shall be in London where General Meetings shall be held.*

So the door on compromise was closed and the meeting at the George Hotel and consequent split became inevitable.

No doubt the RFU regarded the formation of Rugby League as a victory, allowing the true game to be played by those who appreciated the intrinsic value of amateurism and ridding the Union of those who didn't. However, a particular limb of whatever remained of the baby was also thrown away with the bath water and that was the opportunity to develop and change the game itself for the better. Rugby League, faced with a blank sheet of paper, did just that. Its game now depended on money generated through the turnstile and so the interests of the spectator became as important as those of the participant. It identified two elements. First, that if the ball could be kicked into touch at will, the game would only be live for a small proportion of the playing time. Why pay good money to watch ten minutes of rugby when, for the same amount, you could go next door and watch nearly ninety minutes of soccer? Second, that at the point of collision the ball disappeared from view and the game continued without any observable action. They solved the first by allowing no advantage to a side who kicks the ball directly into touch and the second by decreeing that when the player carrying the ball was held, the whistle went to allow the attacking player immediately to resume the game after playing the ball with his foot.

It was also clear that the local crowds preferred running and handling skills to all-in wrestling. To this end, experiments were made as to the ideal number to constitute a team and even the shape of the ball. Eventually, thirteen-a-side was deemed the optimum and although an experiment with the round ball showed it was as easy to handle as the oval version, it encouraged fly hacking and was therefore discarded. Once players could afford time off work to train, they naturally improved their physical strength and stamina. The lineout was no longer necessary to allow the forwards a rest while the ball was being leisurely retrieved. Scrums were seen as a method of restarting a game, which momentarily allowed the talented runners more space, rather than the traditional trial of strength between people of all shapes and sizes.

There is no doubt that, as the new century progressed, Rugby League developed into a more skilful game than its Union counterpart, but it may well be that the changes that were made to encourage a footballing spectacle might have been too much of a shortcut. To avoid the pile-up, any player who was tackled was entitled to keep possession of the ball and it was clear that stalemate would be the eventual outcome. So, the concept of the turn-over after so many tackles was introduced. This is as artificial a concept as any devised by Union officials and it has dictated the shape of the game. At its worst, a side charges forward for five tackles, then boots the ball in the air before the sixth. It seems to me that the essence of rugby football is that the side in possession can keep the ball for as long as it can and exploit that possession in the best way possible. At the same time, the defending side must have a reasonable opportunity to regain possession through its own efforts. At a set piece or the point of collision, the turn-over is possible but never inevitable. This state of affairs demands a more alert attitude to the opportunities at hand and allows the combination of strength and skill to dictate the outcome. Rugby League is the only game I know (unless there is one invented to patronise girls) where if you cock it up you can fall over and start again.

But the Union game suffered the more. As long as the game was being played for the most part by players who were overweight and couldn't be relied on to catch a ball (and as often as not in several inches of mud) there was little need to change the regulations in order to develop the game. But as players became fitter, playing conditions better and coaching demanded a more adventurous style, the limitations of playing to 19th-century rules soon became apparent. The problem that the Union legislators faced was how to change the laws without admitting that Rugby League had it right. As the changes had been clearly driven by the financial desire to make the game a better spectator sport, they were in themselves inherently professional. To copy them was therefore an essential heresy. Fortunately, to aid a struggling Australian Rugby Union, the powers that were had allowed a local dispensation which discouraged the ball from being kicked directly into touch. The Australians thought this would provide a more attractive game both to play and watch and would help them make inroads into the dominance of Rugby League. The effect was remarkable. It moved the Australians from also-rans to arguably the strongest side in the world. More importantly, it allowed the Rugby Union to spread its own 'innovation' without the need to acknowledge the obvious debt.

However, it was not always that easy. I recall a committee meeting in which we had to discuss the effect of 'the changes in the laws on the modern game'. One area in particular exercised the minds of the chosen members. Scrum halves, after an award of a free kick, would quickly tap the ball and run at the nearest opposition forward. Ingrained behavioural patterns meant that the player in question could not resist the opportunity to cause severe physical mayhem on an erstwhile tormentor. As the forward had, inevitably, not retreated the requisite ten metres, another penalty was awarded and the process was repeated. Clearly this smacked of gamesmanship and must be addressed. What was required was an organised hiatus which would allow the defence to retreat and also re-form. Bored with suggestions that were becoming more and more esoteric, I suggested that the player taking the free kick should place the ball on the ground, at the spot indicated by the referee, before heeling it backwards to a member of his own side. For a second or two it was greeted as the perfect solution, until realisation dawned.

A more significant effect of the changes that were made in Rugby League was that they simplified the game. There was no need for a referee and children could organise impromptu games. Ray French, who represented his country at senior level in both codes, remembers his first encounter with floodlit rugby–under the lights of his local street. As the League tackle concentrated on trapping the ball as much as felling the player, it could be played on a hard surface (something specifically forbidden by the RFU) and skills could be developed from an early age. I first discovered the reality of all this when I took an Under 12 XV to Yorkshire to play Normanton Grammar School. This was Rugby League country. The King's boys, steeped in the football of Manchester, had, for the most part, first touched a rugby ball some few weeks previously, but were unbeaten and seemed to have the makings of a pretty decent side. We stood, again for the most part, spectators, as the home team, to the manner born, piled on the points through a variety of switches, loops, miss-moves and whoops of delight. It wasn't that the Macc lads were poor footballers. It was just that their formative learning was inspired by Charlton, Best and Franny Lee and, as a result, they had been quite happy to organise *their* impromptu games in a rather different way.

As a result, if the League looked to recruit from Union, it generally went to South Wales where the game had been played since childhood. Usually, the top Union players like David Watkins and Jonathan Davies were also a great success in League. Now that the Union game has gone open and players with a League background are seizing the financial opportunities on offer, it will be interesting to see if the reverse is true. The three most prominent converts, Henry Paul, Iestyn Harris and Jason Robinson have had mixed fortunes. Robinson has made the England side and would be an automatic selection for a Lions' tour. Paul has had to be content with success at seven-a-side, a game more akin to League with its defensive patterns and attacking options than the full blown fifteen-a-side game. Harris, although he has been picked for Wales, has yet to make the mark he did in the game of his choice. Even Robinson has his critics. His running in open play is electrifying but his ability to read the new game so that he can exploit his talents seems limited. His supporters would say that the Union game does not allow his talents to show to the full and they may well be right. But there is an argument that, as with all games, League and Union are best learned young. A good example of this is a position which on the surface is common to both games: full back. In League, this is the position that will suit the up-and-coming star. His handling and running skills will gain useful yardage and his comparative lack of strength and stamina will not be exploited by having continuously to tackle heavier players. In Union the opposite is true. Being under a high ball when an All Black pack is about to descend is no place for a tyro and in addition to the qualities of Hughes' Crab Jones, he must have the talent and football brain to exploit his position as the *libero*, a combination that usually comes with experience.

So, perhaps these League stars came to the Union game too late. Perhaps they have a different mindset. I have seen scores of young players brought up in a League background play Union at representative level. Some understand that there are less obvious short-term gains in Union and that a lot of apparently profitless activity has to take place before any reward is attained. That an inch gained in the front row can mean that extra yard on the wing. Others do not and quickly lose interest. But, particularly when the grammar schools were in their pomp, players from Wigan to Wakefield flourished in both games, transferring with ease from one code to the other. To watch the coach and players of West Park School, St. Helens, rearranging the traditional public school game to suit their particular skills and strengths was, in its own way, as ground-breaking as watching Puskas & Co destroy the myth of English soccer superiority at Wembley in 1953.

If, between 1960 and 1990, the RFU had harnessed even a small proportion of these talents, I am sure the national side would not, like Nebuchadnezzar, have spent so many years crawling in the long grass of Twickenham or held in thrall by the Dragon of Cardiff. An indication of the depth of talent is shown in the 1986 team list of the Merseyside Schools against Coventry Schools. The Merseyside centres were Kyran Bracken and Bobbie Goulding, both of whom went on to play scrum half for, respectively, England and Great Britain. Apparently, even at District level, neither was good enough to hold down what most people would regard as the pivotal position in the team. When I was coaching the Cheshire side, I would always examine the list of Lancashire players with particular interest. If they came from schools I knew about (schools that played on the same Union circuit as the Cheshire boys) I felt we were in for a fairly even game. If the schools listed contained the likes of Edmund Campion, John Rigby and St John Fisher, I feared the worst. These would be future Rugby League players polishing their skills and CVs and, if allowed to settle, could tear you to pieces.

Such a player was Shaun Edwards. I am not sure where he fits into the Rugby League Pantheon but I suspect even Yorkshiremen must admit he deserves a place near the top. I probably saw more of him as a Union player than most as, at the time he was progressing through the youth ranks, I was a back selector and team manager for the North of England. I say more than most, for the only time Shaun played Rugby Union was at representative level, usually as captain. When he took the field to represent his country against Wales, he had probably played less than a dozen games of the alien code. So much for my theory that a thorough grounding is necessary. I can only plead the exception proves the rule. In fact, it seemed that Shaun didn't attempt to adapt or even acquaint himself too closely with the game. When he was asked if he knew any Union rules, the future captain of Wigan and Great Britain replied, in an accent rarely heard in the coffee shops of Wilmslow, *When ye tackled, let go of it.* Even that piece of knowledge was superfluous as Shaun was rarely tacked. I can't recall a time when he was not on his feet. It is also true to say that at inside centre he didn't inadvertently risk the wrath of the referee by getting too close to the contact area when the other side had the ball. It was with the ball in hand that he was most impressive. I first saw him when Cheshire played Lancashire at Calday RFC. It was a close-fought game, with the home side dominating possession and the Lancashire backs running the ball at every opportunity. Edwards received the ball in his own half and worked his way through the detritus of flankers and centres that Cheshire had strewn in his way. Eventually, he found himself clear, with his winger outside him. He then began, while travelling at speed, a short coaching session for the benefit of his team mate: *Stay where you are, Winger— Come in when I tell you—Keep wide! Keep wide!—Don't come early. Stay wide! Switch when I tell you.* By this time, the remaining Cheshire defender was completely flummoxed, retreating to cover both options. The line approached. *Right, Winger. Now!* The Lancashire winger cut back inside, Edwards appeared to deliver the perfect pass. The Cheshire defence and spectators alike watched the winger hurtling towards the tryline to score between the posts, only to realise, too late, that the ball had never been released and it was in fact Edwards himself who was now touching down by the cornerflag, almost unnoticed.

The remaining county games confirmed that he was a rare talent and he was inevitably selected for the North Trial. At this point, the National selectors descended from Olympus to cast their eye. When the game started, I was standing next to the Chairman of Selectors and informed him about Shaun's playing talents. As befitted his position, he was duly sceptical about parochial praise. Early in the game, Edwards intercepted a pass between fly half and inside centre, sidestepped the full back and scored under the posts. I looked at the Chairman of Selectors. He shook his head. 'Far too risky. If he'd missed, it could easily have been a try at the other end.' A couple of minutes later, Shaun repeated the trick, only this time between inside and outside centre. Then, having made his point, he played sensibly and intelligently until the final whistle. At the selection meeting there was no mention of foolhardiness.

It wasn't that he shone in a sea of mediocrity. Seven of the North backs went on to represent England and completely outplayed London and the South East. At one point in the subsequent trial system, Shaun had not scored and the North were awarded a penalty. As captain, he called to the scrum half who was about to tap and go and the game stopped while he walked across to the mark. It was clear from his body language that he intended to kick at goal. The opposition dutifully filed back. Instead of the expected, Shaun tapped the ball to himself and ran unopposed into the corner. This was, of course, entirely permissible as he had not informed the referee of his intentions. It seemed that, after all, the League player knew more about the Rugby Union laws and ethos than had been supposed. Nevertheless, it was thought by some of the old school to be rather bad form and I was worried it might count against him.

I needn't have. Before the Final Trial, Shaun came to see me to say that he and a fellow trialist had a problem. I assumed an injury of some sort. It turned out that they were not happy to play unless they had previously attended morning Mass. As the Trial kicked off at ten, I thought this might be difficult but took the matter to the Chaiman of Selectors. It turned out there was no problem at all. He was about to attend such a service himself and would be delighted to take the boys with him. By the time they returned and the Final Trial was over, Shaun was able to boast of an unique double by adding the captaincy of the Under 16 England Schools to the already acquired Rugby League equivalent. God, as they say, moves in mysterious ways.

I recount all this not to praise Edwards in particular—his reputation and playing record scarcely needs my addendum—but to show that twenty years ago a 15 year-old lad from a League background had a far greater understanding of the game than most adults who were playing Rugby Union at the time and that it is only in recent years that the Union game has caught up with Rugby League in terms of tactical thinking, mental and physical preparation and general savvy. As a sentimentalist, I would like to see these talents combined. A code to be agreed that would suit all and an administration that puts the game before self interest. As a realist, I recall that King Lear had to go mad and the Duke of Gloucester blind before they realised the folly of their ways.

4

The Laws of the Game *or*
What the Average Player Needs to Know
But Never Dared Ask

If this had been written some ten years ago, it could have emulated Len Shackleton's famous autobiographical chapter entitled 'The Average Director's Knowledge of Football', which was followed by a blank page. By and large, players were encouraged to 'just get on with it' and leave the tricky decisions to the blokes in black. In due course they may have accumulated a series of evocative ripostes such as *Miles Offside! Over the Top! Not Straight, Sir!* or, in final desperation, *Oh! Come On, Ref!* that suggested an intimacy with the various regulations, but in reality they were uttered more in hope than expectation. Even seasoned commentators seemed at times unable to differentiate between 'killing the ball' and 'accidental offside' and retreated into wonderment at the mysteries of front row play or enthusiastic descriptions of rejoicing in clubhouses the length and breadth of the Scottish Borders. *I'll be telling you* was not necessarily followed by the illuminating revelation you might suppose. Then came the radio-mike and the team of three and Lo! the Veil of the Temple was ripped asunder.

The cause of this prelapsarian state was in the main twofold. First, as the players lived in their own little world, they concentrated on only that which directly affected them. There was as little point in a full back discovering the intricacies of illegal binding as there was for a prop to understand the distinction between a knock on and a readjustment. Second, at one stage in the game's evolution a vested interest had developed to make the laws deliberately obscure. If we go back to *Tom Brown's Schooldays*, we see there was no referee. The game was in its origins essentially anarchic. The cries of 'off your side' were more a warning than an instruction. If the culprit failed to heed the advice, no doubt summary and suitably rough justice followed. Indeed, a significant point of sport as a recreation was to avoid the complications of an over-sophisticated society and to return to the primal satisfaction of the struggle where you win or lose.

It was only when sport became an instrument for social control that the schoolmaster (note, master not teacher) took charge. The simplest way to achieve a position of authority is to be the arbiter of the rules.

The natural progression is to take over the legislature and, as a final act, to turn common sense into a mystery. So, education, which was for the most part little more than social ordering, took sport under its wing. Rugby, in particular, with its enforced habit of obedience and deference, was seen as A Good Thing. Why bother with learning the laws when Sir was always right?

But why is the structure of the game so complex and, to some, unnecessarily complicated? The answer probably is part accident, part design. Though even the accident was a design. Back to Tom Brown:

> *Tom's respect increased as he struggled to make out his friend's technicalities, and the other set to work to explain the mysteries of 'off your side', 'dropkicks', 'punts', 'places' and the other intricacies of the great science of football.*

Each public boarding school, to maintain its own individuality and sense of freemasonry, would have its own vernacular which described places, events and school culture. Often newly admitted pupils would have to sit an exam, set not by the academic staff but by the Senior Prefects, which tested this knowledge in particular and the history of the institution in general. This was all part of the 'my school, my college, my club' culture and it was not surprising that they transferred this sense of ownership to the adult world. The ex-pupils of Rugby School seemed determined to make their version of the game the only true one. They even invented the myth of William Webb Ellis, who 'picked up the ball and ran', to assist their case that they were the true inventors of the handling code. It is not surprising that many of the idiosyncrasies that poor Tom thought so confusing found their way into the modern game.

Let us consider three—'touch', 'mark' and 'drop-kick'—all of which appear in the Rugby School version of football. Why is the ball 'in touch' when it crosses the 'touchline'? Again, the patient East explains:

You see this gravel walk running down this side of the playing-ground, and the line of elms opposite on the other? Well, they're the bounds. As soon as the ball gets past them it's out of play and then whoever first touches it, has to knock it straight out among the players-up, who make two lines with a space between them, every fellow going on his own side.

The advantage gained by such a touchdown is shown in the Hughes match report. Old Brooke has the ball.

He stands with the ball in his hand, while the two

sides form deep lines opposite one another: he must strike it straight out between them. The lines are thickest close to him, but young Brooke and two or three of his men are shifting up further, where the opposite line is weak. Old Brooke strikes it out straight and strong, and it falls opposite his brother.

The ball, for once, is in the open and the subsequent rush leads to the only goal of the day.

At one stage it was decided that it was possible for a player to take a quick throw-in, i.e. before the two lines were formed. The laws permit such an act, provided that no other 'person has *touched* [my italics] the ball apart from the player throwing it in'. Were the law-makers reacting to fears of unwarranted interference by a spectator or was it merely an instinctive response to some half-remembered truth? It also explains why at one time when a player was tackled into touch it was still his throw in.

The 'mark' is more obvious. It was integral to the Rugby version of the game that if the attackers, in an attempt to gain ground, propelled the ball too far forward, a defender could catch it and claim a free kick. This was seen as just punishment for an ill-directed hack and a proper reward for anyone brave enough to stand his ground and repel the oncoming hordes.

In order to claim this privilege, three things had to take place simultaneously: a clean catch (no juggling allowed), a heel firmly imprinted in the ground and a vocal ejaculation of the word 'mark'. The purpose of the last two was merely regulatory. The mark in the ground defined the point beyond which the defenders may not advance; the shout to claim the catch demanded immunity from the otherwise legitimate outcome of being trampled upon.

Over time, the regulations changed. It is no longer necessary to mark the spot, as the referee can decide where the ball was caught, and, as a player can only be tackled after he has caught the ball, there seems no need to announce the fact that he has. But the cry remains. It is difficult to explain to the uninitiated that there is a logic at work in much of what happens in rugby. When the game grinds to a halt, apparently because a player has appealed to the patron saint for notaries,* it becomes nigh on impossible.

The drop kick, on the other hand, is self-explanatory. You drop the ball, then kick it. Given the curious shape of the spheroid, it is probably best to do

*Given the professional duties undertaken by notaries, the second gospel writer may also be the patron saint of referees. There are no doubt moments when they feel they need one.

this at the moment the ball hits the ground and before the various laws of mechanics come into play. But what is interesting is why anybody bothered with this elaboration. Why did they not, at all times, punt the ball before it had the chance to bounce? It may be that it was meant to be a challenge. Any one sufficiently skilful to rebound an irregular-shaped object into several inches of mud, then propel it in the required direction with the requisite elevation should be rewarded with three points. The sort of reward that results, in other circumstances, from the performance of a treble somersault with half-pike and twist. On the other hand, it may be that it was at the cutting edge of the modern game. If you study the way today's player approaches a kick at goal, you will observe the rounded shoulders and the hands clasped in front of the body as if trying to hold an object. This mirrors closely the body shape of the player about to drop a goal. Perhaps this body shape encouraged the co-ordination of movement and stillness of the head that is essential if a ball is to be kicked with precision. In other words, for Jonny Wilkinson read Crab Jones. It is interesting to speculate whether any fly half has considered the drop kick as an alternative to the punt when kicking for touch. Particularly if the angle is narrow, the added precision might enable greater length and, if taken from the mark, would make an interesting historical circle.

These terms from yesteryear remain in the game. But how many have been lost? The rulebook has been rewritten so many times that it seems inevitable that some must have been cast into outer darkness or seized upon by the exponents of similar codes. I am not sure how many changes have been made to the rules of soccer, but the only one of any significance I can recall is the restriction on passing the ball back to the goalkeeper. It was a sensible change and probably cut the last strand with the rugby version of football in that there was no longer an opportunity to claim the immunity of the 'mark' when the ball was kicked to you by one of your own players. There may have been others. Certainly there has been a change of emphasis. The definition of violent play seems to have severely restricted the opportunities of regaining possession by the process of kicking the ball with your foot but turned a blind eye to the tugging of shirts. But all this falls into the area of interpretation rather than a change of absolute law.

Rugby Union, on the other hand, has since the last World War decided to make 347 alterations to the code. Actually I have just made up this figure but would happily relinquish any claim to the idea and suggest it as an ideal research project for a PhD in Sports Management. Nevertheless, considerable alterations have been made in every aspect of the game but two. Even the scoring system has vacillated to such an extent that at one time or another it was possible to have an outcome that combined every number from one to infinity. The two immutables are that a ball must be thrown straight into a scrum or lineout and that it must not whilst in play be passed forward. (*NB* These laws only apply to ordinary players. Internationals are, of course, above such trivialities.)

The question is—has stasis arrived or will the laws of the game continue to 'develop'? The former is unlikely. It is now a professional game and there is the same enthusiasm to produce conformity of regulation and interpretation across the globe as there was within the Oxbridge colleges over a century ago. The rule-makers internationally recognise that there is a need to simplify the game for the mass audience. But this is not as straightforward as might be imagined. The game, at the top, is played by super-fit athletes who thrive on continuity and non-stop action. At grass roots level, players still welcome the additional breather of the ball being kicked into a neighbour's garden.

It has to be accepted that Rugby League has already claimed the more obvious crowd-pleasing changes. But Rugby League may have made a mistake. It took a shortcut and ensured continuity by guaranteeing, in the manner of American Football, possession for a defined period of time. Rugby Union has the opportunity to frame the laws so that they allow a passage of play that is not only continually active but also consistently under threat. It is important that in making any changes account is taken that the knife-edge of capture or escape, disaster or triumph is the fundamental point of interest in a spectator sport. The more balanced the outcome, the more exciting it is. Sports like basketball have, to the casual spectator, abandoned the midfield struggle and reduced the game to the skill of the shooter. Even the world game, soccer, has given up the challenge in favour of a cat-and-mouse approach. Currently, most legislative changes and refereeing interpretation seem to be concentrating on the policing of the tackle area— and rightly so. However, there are other opportunities for the ball to be turned over and it would add to the game if, for example, the strike against the head again surfaced at international matches. The decisions that are made now will be critical to the way in which the game develops and eventually appeals—or not— to a wider audience than those who have previously played the game.

But if Rugby Union is to support the idea of physical confrontation as the essence of the game, then another and contradictory question raises its head. If there is to be a struggle, there has to be a degree of violence and the consequence of possible injury. We have to assume that the laws will only allow a degree of violence that is acceptable but this opens a door. The problem lies when violence becomes illegal or gratuitous. Over the years this has been controlled by an unwritten code of gentlemanly conduct which, by and large, means that if you are going to hit someone, you hit someone your own size and offer no complaint when the compliment is returned. There is the famous story of an International prop from the West Country who at the first scrum always took the opportunity to punch his immediate opponent. As he explained, 'If nothing happened, I knew I was in for an easy game. If the punch was returned, I knew I was in for a good one.' This form of self-regulation was generally accepted and for the most part unseen.

The whole business of handbags at five paces and the 'naughty schoolboy' syndrome of playing the referee to see what you can get away with was endemic in the game and, if not particularly uplifting, was part of the culture you bought into if you chose to play. Then came professionalism and the television replay. Cheating and illegal violence assumed different proportions. If you are playing for your mortgage rather than recreation, then different factors are at work. Previously, affairs had been regulated by individuals who had the good of the game at heart and would impose a firm code of discipline to deter wrongdoing. But now, when clubs—and therefore to a degree the game—are owned by entrepreneurs, it is less likely that similar scruples will apply. On top of this is the attitude of the television presenter. Where once the occasional flying boot would have passed unnoticed in the stands or, at most, brought a roar of disapproval from those near enough to see it, now it is viewed from every angle in slow motion, actual speed and whatever other technical trick the producer can dream up. Of course, like most reporting of violence, it is done under the umbrella of seeking the truth but it is in fact little more than rabble-rousing and makes good copy. If the truth was all that was at stake, the evidence could be shown in private to dispassionate judges. One of the strengths of rugby was that, regardless of the perceived injustice, you just got on with the game and did not stand about arguing the toss. Soccer and its supporters have gone down the road of comparing a Saturday afternoon stroll in the park to a struggle against the Antichrist and it is not surprising that people have been killed as a result. Agree or not with this earlier approach, it is nevertheless important that those who control the game are seen to keep violence and the exploitation of violence in check. Otherwise, parents will start to feel the same trepidation on watching their sons set off for mini rugby that they once reserved for the sight of their daughters disappearing on the pillion of a motorbike.

In the light of that last remark, it is also important to keep a close check on the effects of legitimate violence. The track record in this direction has been good. Considerable work has been done on the potential damage to participants in the scrum and the laws are now framed to offer the maximum safeguard. In particular, it has been recognised that there is a need for differing legislation to distinguish between the adult and the growing body. As a result, the scrummage is much more stable and less likely to collapse. The tackle is another point of collision where injury might well occur and as it is the essence of the game physically and psychologically, it would be impossible to abolish or even seriously limit it. However, its very seriousness makes it paradoxically safer. A player knows that if he is in possession of the ball, he is a legitimate target for physical attack and will prepare himself accordingly. It is usually when he is caught off-balance or unaware, as in the late tackle, that he is likely to be hurt.

It is because of this that I consider that one of the most dangerous moments in the game, and one that should be carefully examined, is the act of scoring a try, when a player dives or burrows for the line. Because of the potential reward, he may fail to safeguard himself, or even voluntarily risk something he would have otherwise avoided. Perhaps the time has come for the act of scoring a try to be reconsidered. If the law were changed so that a try may be awarded only when a player carrying the ball is on his feet and wholly within the in-goal area before touching down, there might be some interesting repercussions. I realise that the dive for the corner is one of the more spectacular sights in the game, but grown men scrabbling around on all fours is one of the less. There could well be an end to five-metre fever and an incentive to move the ball into spaces where attackers could cross the line in a less simian fashion. There would be mutterings in the catch'n'drive/push-over scrum department but this would not necessarily be a bad thing. It all depends on how you think the game should be played in the 21st century. At the very least, it might encourage a variety of tactics at the set pieces close to the line.

Stasis is unlikely. Coaches will always try to find loopholes. Players will always cheat if they can get away with it. Legislators will continue to play catch-up, at times unwittingly creating problems for themselves to solve. If roll-on, roll-off substitution is allowed to counter the abuse of the blood-bin, will every side have an attacking and defensive fly half? The questions go on. Should the need for a specialist kicker ruin the shape of a side? Should all kicks be in front of goal? Ultimately, do countries that play on hard pitches in warm climes want the same laws as those who play in harsher northern climates?

Whatever the cause of all these complications, one outcome is certain—the rise in importance of the referee. For the game of Rugby Union to be played in

its evolved form, it became obvious that an independent arbiter was essential. It is a commonplace for after-dinner speakers to thank the match officials 'without whom the game would not be possible'. This was not always so. Usually any dispute would first be resolved by the two captains. Later, inter-school matches often featured a member of staff on each side who would ensure fair play and a proper result. Eventually the adult ceased to play himself and took over the role of host and organiser. And so the referee was born. But what sort of person wants to take on such a job? As is usually true, no general answer will suffice. In fact, the role has altered quite considerably over the years and may well have attracted different types at different times.

In the beginning, the referee was probably someone whose good nature could be relied upon to help others enjoy themselves. The kindly adult who would give up his own time and interests for a common good. The schoolmaster who ran and refereed the Junior Colts B XV was the same bloke who organised the Stamp Club or Model Railway Society. He saw it as part of the job to encourage and support the enthusiasms of others. In return, he assumed that the players would accept whatever interpretation of events he chose to enforce without question and with suitable deferential compliance.

But amongst that group of philanthropists there were those who saw the opportunity as a challenge. They took pleasure in an intimate knowledge of the laws of the game and would measure their success in the accuracy of their enforcement. Like the players, they would pride themselves on having a good game. At worst, they were pedants ticking their way through the rulebook as if they were collecting train numbers. At best, they developed a rapport with the players, using the advantage law to its full. They were, of course, dictators, the sole judge of law and fact, but for the most part the benevolent version of that ilk. Again, players generally accepted the decisions without question and were immediately penalised if they didn't.

Out of this group has grown a further type. Not content with their role as policemen, they sought to become members of the judiciary. They saw their role not merely as the apprehender of felons but as learned interpreters of the legislature. The law of the land demands that each individual should take reasonable care not to harm his neighbour; the law of rugby demands that after a player is tackled he must immediately release the ball. The terms 'reasonably' and 'immediately' are generally understood but the exact perimeters of the terms may well alter owing to circumstances and so have to be interpreted in the light of events. As the Law Lords can and do shape social behaviour by their verdicts, so a group of referees might well be able to shape the way the game is played in the future. The professional game is developing such a group and future aspirants may well be attracted by the power that is on offer. Such is this power that it is common practice for coaches to interview the referee to see how he is going to interpret certain areas of the laws and shape their game plan accordingly. There is no other game where the official has such control and whose philosophy or even whim—rather than error of judgment—can determine the outcome of a match. A law is open to interpretation; a rule is not. Whatever is the ideal of the ultimate arbiter is difficult to determine, but one thing is certain, the Honorary Chairman of the Stamp Club has had his day.

5

Loony Left Saves English Rugger!!!

It would have taken a far-seeing sports reporter to produce this particular tabloid headline. But it was on the cards until the Labour Government was ousted and the Tories, rather than it, raised the school leaving age from 15 to 16. As it was, nobody noticed and we didn't even get the admittedly more alliterative but somehow less telling

MILK SNATCHER MAKES AMENDS!

Of course, ROSLA had the obvious benefit to both parties of lowering unemployment at a stroke, but what neither they, the sporting press nor the RFU seemed to realise was the effect this educational decision would have on the development of rugby in England, or how the denizens of Twickers would be eternally grateful to the educational free-thinkers who believed in equal opportunity for all.

Up to that point, the age group of the first attempt to produce an English Schools side was under 15 at 1st September. The players that were selected were inevitably those who were big for their age. Players who, because of an early growth spurt, could out-physique more talented but less maturely developed opponents were favoured in the dog-eat-dog form of selection that took place at the time. They were a team of the short-term anatomically advantaged and, not surprisingly, few of them progressed to higher things. In addition, the Under 15s were always re-garded by the Schools' Union as a poor relation. A sop to those who were forced to abandon school at the earliest possible age. Any absence of continuity did not seem to be a matter for over-concern. In-deed, many of the major public schools regarded the whole procedure as something of an irrelevance.

At a time when it was assumed that the majority of International players would come through the in-dependent schools system and the Varsity match was in effect the Final England Trial, there seemed little point in encouraging youth rugby across the social spectrum or introducing a policy of player develop-ment. Indeed, the gap between Under 15 and the next age group at Under 19 was so great that continuity of any sort was highly unlikely. In truth, international schoolboy rugby was something of an indulgence. An Under 19 side would consist for the most part of boys who found themselves in the third year sixth either because of Oxbridge entry ambitions or as a result of being unable to follow the normal progress on the escalator of secondary education. However, in 1974, the Rugby Football Schools' Union decided to follow the national trend and raise the age of the junior International side from Under 15 to Under 16. The motives behind this change were various. Some, again, saw it as the last chance for a working-class boy before entering the real world of employment. Others knew that at this age group a sea change occurred and players identified as talented at 16 were more likely to stay the course than their predecessors. The immediate result was that a flow path was established between the two age groups and when, ten years later, the Union decided to lower the age of the senior side to Under 18, players first identified and then developed by the Schools' Union started to form the nucleus of an élite group that went on to play rugby at the highest levels. Today Clive Woodward could, with every confidence, field an International side that had represented England Schools at one time or another.

Because of this success and particularly because those involved began to see a direct connection between their efforts at youth level and the ultimate outcome at senior level, the ERFSU started to become more proactive than reactive. Schemes were launched that allowed all players a better opportunity to show their ability and development. In addition, the process of selection became less rudimentary. There were still problems. Administratively, the Groups at 16 and 18 were run separately and there was only a token connection between them. The latter ran a system that had its own Five Nations competition, with regular tours abroad, and saw no need to change what was essentially a comfortable and self-serving situation. Indeed, there were 18 Group committee members who felt that Under 16 rugby infringed on their province and that the junior side should revert to Under 15, i.e. where it belonged.

As it happened, circumstances played into the objectors' hands. Wales, who had previously lost merely eleven games out of eighty against England at Under 15 level, won only two of the next eight when the game was played between sides a year older. The Welsh reaction was to withdraw from the fixture until they felt they had produced a suitable system to select and develop a team at that age level. The fixture resumed a decade later, though rugby historians might consider what effect that hiatus had on the comparative strengths of the two nations. But, in the short term, the result was that Engand at 16 level had no one to play—Wales had gone and France, at the same time, preferred to develop younger players at provincial rather than national level. The best that was on offer were games against Holland, Spain, Portugal and Italy—fixtures that were perceived by some as well below par. The nadir arrived when it seemed no opposition could be found and the selected XV were reduced to playing a President's XV. The old guard's synchronised display of raising eyebrows, shrugging shoulders, rolling eyes and clicking tongues would have been awarded a perfect ten in any gymnastic competition.

Yet out of such adversity sprang a real advantage. The President's XV was in effect a second team. The match was a close encounter and proved that the difference between a player selected or rejected on the day could, in many cases, be very slight. Although the freakish element of selection at 15 had been considerably reduced, there is no doubt that differences in levels of maturation would and do still occur. As an example, I remember a selectorial decision I had to make between two inside centres. Both were talented players, with one the more robust but slightly less skilful. Recalling a recent demolition job performed on a similarly slight player by the Welsh back row, I went along with the decision, against my better judgment, to pick the heavyweight. My excuse for my pusillanimity was that the other could be accommodated in the A team, where he could develop at his own pace. Both players are currently playing in the Premiership, but it is the A team player who has attained International status. By running two teams, the 16 Group secured a group of fifty players who could form the base of an élite pyramid.

However, for the Schools' Union to operate effectively, two areas had to be addressed. First, the two groups at 16 and 18 had to work more closely together and, second, the Union had to dispel the myth that selection was a closed shop and that the school you went to was as important as your skill as a player. In other words, the belief that the ERFSU was the RFU writ small. As with all myths, there is some truth and anecdotal evidence abounds. David Storey, author of *This Sporting Life*, recalls how as a boy he played through a series of state school trials. At this early stage, he felt that the better players were chosen on merit. Eventually, the selected fifteen were pitched against a side of matching kit and accents who were in due course and, to Storey, with a sense of inevitability, selected en bloc for the County. He returned to Rugby League. Of course, it is easy to blame your own inadequacies on the partisanship of selection. Nevertheless, justice must be seen to be done and therefore any process must be open and transparent.

The Union was very fortunate that at this time Dennis Shuttleworth was elected President and Ron Davidson, a man who fully understood the frustrations of the 16 Group, Vice President. Between them, they not only closed the gap between the 16 and 18 Groups and but also persuaded them to act in concert. Moreover, in the process, they got rid of excessive forelock tugging to the public school headmasters and moved the junior side a few paces above the salt. Most importantly, the Constitution was changed so that Divisions could elect their own selectors, nominate coaches and appoint team managers, thus developing a pathway which all could follow and, more importantly, understand. I always enjoyed the Executive Meetings that discussed the subject. As an exercise in political persuasion, they were wondrous to behold. Propositions from the chair that were initially considered totally unacceptable became, through a process of withdrawal and re-presentation, eventually palatable. Committees that had been at arm's length came together to discuss a common policy. Irrefutable truths were modified. Entrenched positions were surrendered. Everything in the English garden seemed rosy.

But English rugby would not be English rugby if everything ran like clockwork. As soon as it appeared that the Schools' Union was dominating the selection process, the Clubs lodged their complaint. Traditionally, the introduction of the game had been through lessons at school and the Clubs had taken little interest in developing players at this early stage, assuming a steady flow from school to club. As many of the Clubs were Old Boy Associations, this assumption was reasonably founded.

However, as a result of the demise of the grammar schools and, in particular, the teachers' strike of the 1980s, it became clear that this source would soon dry up. Consequently, rugby clubs started to form their own mini and junior sections. Many of the players who were to progress to representative honours learned their rugby in this manner rather than at school and the Clubs, quite reasonably, objected when the Schools' Union claimed them as their own. They argued that the Clubs should have an equal opportunity to select a representative side and that this should be a proper pathway to senior rugby.

This was all right in theory but tended to founder in practice. To allow such a situation to flourish, it was essential that all individual clubs ran age-group teams on a regular basis. They found it very difficult to do this on the traditional Saturday as a significant number of their players had commitments to school rugby and, as often as not, independent school rugby at that. In addition, it was also the policy of the ERFSU to discourage boys from playing twice in 48 hours. The Clubs protested that it was they who had introduced the boys to the game and that the player should be allowed to choose which team he played for—school or club. The RFU considered. As the members probably assumed that 'schools' meant the type of institution they themselves had attended, they dutifully sided with the wishes of the HMC and decreed that the headmaster's decision should be final and, in effect, the school should have first call and, what is more, that only boys of whom the school approved were to be eligible for representative honours.

The clubs were upset. No doubt fuelled by memories of childhood injustice, they felt the whole affair was a conspiracy. They presented a case that the Schools' Union was a spent force, staffed by an ageing and élitist group of reactionaries. They argued that the real hope of driving the game forward lay with the clubs, who, even against the odds, could present Clive Woodward with a XV that would rival anything that the Schools could produce. A combination of Junior Clubs, who were no longer willing to kowtow to every Twickenham whim, and Senior Clubs, who wanted the playing side of the game to be organised on more professional lines, led to the formation of the inevitable committee which had, among other matters, to examine this issue.

The Horner Committee was formed and a decision eventually reached. There was no doubt that the process was thorough; not a corner of the land was left unturned. However, I was not particularly impressed with the agenda. I felt one of the key questions that had to be addressed in a modern professional game was how Rugby Union might tap into the stream of talented youngsters who had traditionally played League. Those with most experience in this matter were the North Division of the ERFSU.

It knew there was an important group of potential England players who might fall between the proposed stools because they neither attended Rugby Union-playing schools or were members of a Rugby Union club. But the only consultation in which the Division was officially involved was an apologetic afterthought on a wet evening in Ossett. By this time, minds seemed to have been made up and the inquisitors appeared more interested in the time of the next train south than examining any contrary evidence.

Not surprisingly, the product was no better. In another Solomonic moment, the committee reached for the cleaver. Under 18 representative rugby was to be divided between boys who attended 'rugby-playing schools' and those who didn't. If you attended the former, you were available for selection for the ERFSU XV, if not, the RFU Clubs XV. Of course, this begged the question as to when a school was a 'rugby-playing school'. Various formulae were suggested, taking into account number of terms played, nature of the opposition and range of age-group sides. In one glorious moment, a regulation was proposed that would have actually excluded Rugby School itself. Eventually, the County Schools' Union was given a list of schools from which they could choose their

Under 18 side. Some Counties chose to ignore this, explaining that it seriously undermined their own development programme of Youth rugby. In Northumberland, for example, it was thought impossible to produce two sides of reasonable quality if the split was rigidly adhered to. In the opinion of those who knew what was happening, both in schools and clubs, the development of rugby in the county had a much greater chance of success if the status quo was maintained. What might happen to work in Middle Earth and the Mystical County of Middlesex would not necessarily meet with similar success under the shadow of St James' Park. As had so often happened, the front end of the pantomime horse had not consulted the rear.

The 16 Group argued that, as the law of the land demanded that all boys must remain at school in their age group, they were therefore, *ipso facto*, schoolboys and so must, regardless of background, be available for selection for the Schools' representative sides. This argument was, given a moment's thought, entirely spurious, but it says a good deal about the state of affairs that it remained unchallenged. In fact, the lack of opposition appeared to lay bare the truth. The people who were staging the protest and demanding change were not so much the clubs at large, who were trying to protect their home-grown players, but a small proportion of power-seekers who now found themselves in no man's land. This group consisted of the committee men, selectors and coaches who had previously run and controlled an International XV that was effectively defunct: the Colts, an Under 19 side of early school leavers. Now, because of the social change that had encouraged students to stay on into the Sixth Form, they had been left with an empty barrel. They saw Horner as an opportunity to reassert their power base in the struggle to control youth rugby. What is more, experience had taught them that it was in their interests if the Schools' Union did the early spadework of player identification and they then took over their lot at the age of 17. Hence, there was no real pressure to examine the rights of clubs to control the destiny of their Under 16 players. In fact, such club talent unearthed by the current system was, as often as not, poached by the independent schools offering scholarships into their Sixth Form. Once again, the clubs saw what they regarded as rightfully theirs disappearing from under their noses. The result of the Horner decision was to bring even more rancour on to the youth scene.

Despite the politics, there were genuine problems that had to be addressed if the matter of young player development was left in the hands of the clubs. It was argued that too often the people involved in coaching and organising junior teams at this level were parents who had a vested interest only as long as their offspring were playing. Sadly, this parental interest waxes and wanes with the response of the child. When son finds alternative amusements, there can seem little point in Dad turning up to coach a bunch of other people's kids. He feels that he has done his bit and leaves the club effectively in the lurch. Even if the child continues to express interest, there is a tendency for club coaches to go up the age groups with a successful team. Success attracts support but less successful age groups can be left unaided and soon disappear. It is very easy for even a successful group to disintegrate. The team loses key players, the squad shrinks in number and defeat follows, with consequent further defection. Unlike a school, the club, relying on volunteers, has no infrastructure to control this situation. Teams collapse, players lose interest and the more talented and committed look elsewhere for their sporting opportunities. The club may try to plug the gap but often with undesirable results—players playing in teams outside their age group or, worse, run by adults who for a variety of reasons are not particularly suited to the job in hand.

I suspect that the enthusiastic support for mini rugby both by fathers and sons gave the clubs a false impression of the situation. At face value, the popularity of such schemes indicated that they had struck a rich vein of future players and supportive club members. In reality it was probably just a reflection of the contemporary social fabric. Dads were only too keen to take their child to the club. It was an opportunity to fulfil a paternal duty, with the added advantage of meeting like-minded fathers around the bar once the morning session had finished. Small boys were willing accomplices. It was their opportunity to fall around in the mud and splash about in the bath, with the odd bit of unpunished gratuitous violence thrown in.

So if, as the French have it, the Schools weren't up to it and the Clubs weren't on to it, what was the RFU to do? The current suggestion is to hand over the running of Youth rugby to a professional group of Regional Development Officers who will be responsible for developing élite squads that will form the base of future representative teams. This seems an eminently sensible solution at face value. A successful national team is essential to the financial success of the game. A system where accountable individuals are responsible for that outcome is to be preferred to a system that relies on the hit or miss appearance of the volunteer. But it does have its drawbacks. The cost to replicate professionally the services of scores of unpaid enthusiasts would be enormous, not only in salary terms but also in underpinning the administrative expenses that are often swallowed in educational and personal accounts. The goodwill of the amateur who is to an extent willing to finance his hobby is still essential. If, in a fit of pique, they were simultaneously to take their bats home, they would be very costly to replace.

A quick look at the North Division, at 16 Group only, gives an idea of the scale. Local schoolteachers and club members nominate players to be selected for County representation. In a county the size of Yorkshire, this could be hundreds of individuals. Local trials have to be organised and an initial weeding process takes place. Once this has happened, a selection programme consisting of trials and development days will eventually, over a series of weekends, produce a County side. This in turn plays the other Northern Counties and, as a result, 50+ players in the North of England are identified and invited to attend a development weekend. There, the players' ability is assessed and a Final Trial is arranged. Aided by the England Selectors, a North squad is chosen and a further development weekend takes place before the National process begins. On top of this, there is an administrative arm that organises venues, kit, travel, etc. This process, which begins in September and does not finish until after the New Year, involves a considerable number of man-hours and a reasonable degree of logistical expertise and would be expensive to replace. There are those who argue that this degree of grading is unnecessary but it is the Schools' experience, at least in the North of England, that this is the only fair way to ensure that every player is able to have an equal chance.

But there is more to it than money. Rugby Union is a taught game. It could never have evolved without the inspiration of those, whether at school or club, who teach it. If such people feel that the better players are being removed from their set-up or, worse, that players are being pulled in a variety of directions, they may feel the effort is not worth the candle. There is no doubt in my mind that if the game ceased to be taught, it would die out within a generation or, at best, retreat into the small pools of exclusive existence whence it came. The very nature of the game means that the talented player in the early stage of his development requires the hewers of wood and fetchers of water both to play with and against. This infrastructure is already fragile and is threatened by the inability of anyone to grasp the real nettle.

And that is, the game is already divided into three parts. The RFU wants to set up an élite pathway. The individual schools want to maintain their playing prestige. The clubs, for their very survival, need to recruit and keep players. It does not require a visit to the Oracle at Delphi to forecast the outcome. Any player with even the most modest of aspirations is likely to be pulled three ways. A not untypical week for such a player was discussed at a recent County Schools' meeting which was attended by RFU and Club representatives. The programme read: *Monday* RFU training via Active Sports; *Tuesday* School Player Development; *Wednesday* Club Training; *Thursday* School match preparation; *Saturday* School Match; *Sunday* (often without 24 hours respite) Club Match; *Monday*... It's little wonder if he slopes off to the pub on Friday. Quite apart from the academic repercus-

sions, there is also evidence that such a programme destroys his enthusiasm for the game and, when demands spill over the natural boundaries of the season and insist on attendance at summer camps, to the detriment of other recreational activities, you are asking young players to make decisions about their future without proper guidance. In my experience, when you offer the young a series of alternatives, their first reaction is to try to achieve them all and then, when they realise they can't, close their eyes to reality and eventually do none.

So what should be done? First, the RFU, despite its obvious reservations, should entrust youth development and the construction of élite pathways to the Schools' Union. Only when the player is at the tertiary educational stage should the RFU, like other institutions of further education, come into play. To narrow a student's options at an earlier stage is against both common sense and educational opinion. Of course, all coaches like to embalm their imprint as early as possible and the pragmatic arguments against this Jesuit principle are not easy to sustain. But I feel that there are a number of special pleadings that can be made in the case of Rugby Union.

First, the existing Schools' system has produced

not only the backbone of currently the best side in the world but also a muster of players to support a successful league programme. It has, in the process, encouraged the less talented to commit themselves to the game both as players and supporters. The latter group is not to be underestimated, as an oversubscribed Twickenham is the measure of the game's success. While there is no doubt that many fine players escape the net or are not even available for selection at this stage in their life, the number of good players that are identified and selected for international representation are sufficient to act as a benchmark against which others can be judged.

Second, schools do and will for the foreseeable future exist and the vast majority of individuals attend them. It would make sense for a number of these institutions to be identified as centres within the community which would offer the opportunity for all players in the district to receive the proper level of coaching and playing experience. The RFU could support these institutions in an appropriate manner and through a series of courses and seminars keep local coaches in touch with current thinking. In particular, they could attack the root of the problem and pay for relief cover if teachers had to attend trials, matches, etc, in school time.

Third, you would not have to reinvent the wheel. In supporting the Schools' Union, I do not hold it up as a paragon. It has made mistakes both in assessing the players' needs and in finding the best structure but it has had the opportunity of addressing them. In particular, parents and players can understand the set-up and see a clear pathway to the pinnacle of the England side. As a condition, it would have to ensure that its structure could include all potential players and tap into the talent which is currently the preserve of Rugby League, or sports where the stopwatch rather than prejudice is the judge.

Fourth, those involved in running school rugby are the true professionals when dealing with the vocational aspirations of youth. They know and understand children and are unlikely to mistake a 16 year-old standing six feet, three inches tall and weighing sixteen-and-a-half stone for a man. Indeed, if Performance Directors mistakenly treat such a frame as such, they may well find their protégés are rather shorter-lived than they imagined.

And fifth, unlike some games, it is probably better to develop the élite rugby player when his brain and emotional temperament have sufficiently matured. Let him master the skills in his teens and learn the subtleties and suffer the knocks in his twenties. There is much evidence that sides that win World Cups are old and wise and it would be a pity if the available talent was always burnt out, physically and mentally, at 25. Our present society is being driven by Performance Objectives, often to the detriment of the actual activity itself. It would be particularly ironic if the one sport that came so late to the table did not at least take notice of the folly of others in general and Association Football in particular.

Sixth, and the value you place on this defines where you stand, does the game wish to retain any of the elements that its amateur precursors valued so much? That it is still as much a recreation as a job. That it should not extinguish other opportunities. That because of its intrinsically violent nature it must be self-disciplined and self-contained and sustain a code that respects the efforts of your opponent. If so, the game is better placed in the hands of those who have a more rounded and balanced view of the future of the child than the touchline marauders who urge their offspring on with cries of *Kill him, Jimmy. Kill!*

6

Dirty Dancing

What do you see in rugby?
    I suspected that the question stemmed more from politeness than interest, but a reply seemed necessary:
It's difficult to say.
The eyes of the literary lady started to wander. So, grasping at a passing straw:
I am quite taken by the unlikely combination of violence and ballet.
The initial supposition turned out to be, for the most part, correct since subsequent conversations tended more to Prokofiev than punch-ups.
Like most off-the-cuff responses, my remark had more sound-bite than substance but, as a definition, it does embrace the two extremes of the coaching philosophy. Either consciously or unconsciously, the coach must decide whether he is going to encourage his players to bully or to dance. Most coaches would argue that they do both but in my experience there is

always an instinctive tendency one way or the other and the selection and tactics of the team reveal this reality. Any coach who does not select a talented flanker because he is too small, or chooses a kicking fly half over a running fly half, is making a statement as to how the game should be played. As the point of any game is to win, it also indicates a belief as to the best way of achieving that result.

Up to 1970, bullying was in vogue, backed by the apparent invincibility of, in turn, New Zealand and South Africa. New Zealand would rely on superior fitness and carefully co-ordinated effort to keep control of the ball and wear down the opposition. The ball rarely went beyond scrum half and, if it did, it was kicked into a position where the back row were either certain to retrieve it or, alternatively, instigate a ruck which swept through less organised sides with enormous power and determination. South Africa, because they played and trained in dry, warm conditions, were prepared to move the ball wide, confident that their muscular superiority could maintain possession and make severe inroads over the gain line. Moreover, this also gave them the opportunity, when playing the British Lions, to pinpoint any weakness in their opponents' ball-playing strength. A talented fly half would be remorselessly hunted down, knocked off his game and, if possible, incapacitated. 'Nothing trivial, I trust,' as I have more than once heard a coach of this ilk remark when the opposition star player sinks to the floor clutching a vital part of his anatomy.

The English have tended to vacillate. At times they have tried to maintain the Corinthian ethic, at others, when the force was with them, they attempted to emulate the colonials. An interesting example of the former is the story of an English lock playing for the Lions against New Zealand. Inevitably, he was deliberately and violently fouled at a lineout. His response, after dusting himself down, was to offer his hand to the perpetrator. Fearing a trick, this was nervously accepted. Noting the bewilderment of the Irish prop standing next to him, the Englishman explained, 'You wouldn't understand, old boy. I was trying to make him feel a cad.' Far less interesting is when the English abandon any pretence that they are involved in a handling game and select fly halves whose only attribute is that they kick the length of the park and inside centres who won't or can't pass.

The Celts studied the laws carefully and developed a game plan based on the guerrilla warfare that

had served their ancestors so well. Although outnumbered, they were more skilful than the relatively clumsy Anglo Saxons and thus could secure victories that were both memorable and satisfying. Their problem is that, like certain red wines, they do not travel too well and tend to end up in a bit of a mess in the hands of the real gorillas. The French, of course, were and are the French. Much energy and direction is still lost on deciding whether *élan* or *éclat* should decide this year's style of play. The Australians were in financial difficulties and had still to persuade a sufficient number of adult players to choose Union over League or Rules as the preferred game of footy.

So, up to 1970, each country developed its own style of play that reflected the national temperament and geographical playing conditions. This style was not so much coached as ingrained. The extreme example was in New Zealand, where a pattern of forward play was introduced from the age of seven and carried out through the remainder of a player's career with ruthless ferocity. It is obviously a gross generalisation to say the Welsh favoured a running game, the Scottish a spoiling game, the Irish 'gave it the lash', etc, but there is a sufficient element of truth in the assertion. Sufficient to develop a national philosophy and a mode of play that young players would emulate and, more importantly, assimilate. That may be the reason why foreign coaches don't do so well when asked to travel. They assume a culture that doesn't exist and ignore one that does.

An interesting example of this was a recent article in *The Guardian* on the Sale Sharks fly half/centre, Jos Baxendell. The main thrust of the article was whether the likes of Jonny Wilkinson would last as long in the game as the Sale player (237 first team appearances and counting). But in the general discussion a significant point emerged. Jos, in the course of his career, had been coached by a Welshman, Paul Turner, and two Kiwis, John Mitchell and Glen Ross. He thought of the first that he was a genius and of the Kiwis not a lot. Mitchell, of course, has been entrusted with the job of leading the All Blacks to their first World Cup win since all teams have been available or taken the competition seriously. It is unlikely that Turner will be asked to perform a similar role. However, Baxendell's choice is not surprising. As a young player, he had been brought up to believe that *(a)* the main purpose of the game was to get the ball into the hands of the ball-players, *(b)* possession rather than position was the crucial factor in any decision to launch an attack and *(c)* when faced by the opposition's back division you saw not four defenders but three spaces through which you or a team-mate could run.

At one stage, then, it seemed that each country would stick to and polish its evolved game. All except for poor old England. It had no single game. A match between two southern public school sides had little in common with a game between two grammar school sides in St Helens. It was, as Ray French once remarked, 'rapiers and cudgels'. Any selection of a national side would bring together a plethora of playing preferences, usually with disastrous results. The criticism that England, with its greater playing base, should do better is spurious if the fly half comes from the Forest of Dean and the centres from the M62 corridor. In fact, England tended to do well when selection, fairly or unfairly, favoured a particular region.

Then, in 1971, a curious thing happened. The Lions toured New Zealand and won the series. But it was not so much the victory that mattered. There is no doubt that the touring party contained a number of exceptional players. Also, the weather was kind and allowed them to play the game that they wanted.

What was curious was the effect it had on British rugby at large. As the heart of the party was Welsh, they were the major beneficiaries, but throughout the land, aided by a ball that no longer resembled a wet bar of soap, a new running game developed. Developed to such an extent that it produced the legendary Barbarian match against New Zealand in 1973 and, more importantly, in the Lions Tour to South Africa in 1974 it completely destroyed the myth of Springbok invincibility. British, or at least Celtic, rugby seemed to have taken a seat at the top table. The English also prospered, albeit in patches, but the abolition of the grammar schools slowed the progress and it was to be more than a quarter of a century before those patches were sewn together into anything resembling a garment.

Why did it happen? There may have been a variety of little reasons but there was one major contributor. John Dawes, the captain of the 1971 Touring side, organised an International Players' Conference in which 'he and some of the key members of his victorious team would discuss the latest trends in Rugby Union football and offer the fruits of their experience'. The conference took place at the Polytechnic of North London in July 1971 and the papers and subsequent question-and-answer session were published in a book entitled *The Lions Speak*.

The title is significant. The Lions speak, not roar. This was no act of triumphalism but a scholarly and informed assessment of how matters stood. Each of the speakers was an expert in his field. They explained not only the arts of their respective positions but how they exploited the weaknesses of the opposition. At last there was a common curriculum for coaches throughout the land and a belief that possession rather than field position was the key to success. Not that tactical kicking was eschewed—it was seen as an important way to exploit possession. The game was still football but, for the first time since William Webb Ellis introduced his own 'dispensation', handling was seen to be on a par. There followed, particularly in Wales, a glorious decade where fly halves glided through gaps, wingers counter-attacked from under their own posts and centres drew the defensive sting for full backs to thunder through the created space.

But it was the final speaker who really made the difference. Carwyn James, the coach of the tour party, explained his philosophy. His essential attitude is shown at the start of his talk, when he described the try that Barry John, the King, scored against New

Zealand Universities:

> *There was a scrummage on the 25. The ball came out to Barry. He moved the top half of his body right without moving his feet at all, and one or two back-row forwards went the wrong way. Then he moved left, right, left and under the sticks. Poetry!*
>
> *The try was received with a bit of a hush by the New Zealand spectators, not because of bad sportsmanship, but because it was not in their line of country. In their pattern, Barry's opposite number would kick the ball high into the box, or kick a high up and under and the spectators would be on the edge of their seats, loving it, enjoying it! This was rugby football! Put the ball in the air, let's have eight men going after this ball and let us feel the thump!*

It was the word 'poetry' that was the key. Perhaps a touch inflated, but sufficient to distinguish his view of the game from its crude and violent beginnings.

His training sessions caused the locals to stare in disbelief. Whereas their heroes worked hard running, rucking, rucking, running, the Lions sessions were a much more casual affair. Little groups chatting, trying something, chatting. A tuck here, a trim there. The highlight occurred on the Wednesday afternoon before the final test. Carwyn had been working with the forwards at one end of the field, the backs surrounded by an enormous crowd at the other. The coach excused himself, saying that he wanted to see what the backs were up to. He expected they were probably playing football. To his delight (though he suspected they had seen him coming) they were practising a scissors move that had caused the Lions such defensive difficulties in a recent match. The move consisted of a scissors back towards the pack, an expected ploy, followed by a scissors back into open play. John Dawes had been trying to build upon it. In the end, to the astonishment and horror of their audience, they had a move that included seven sets of scissors. With only a couple of days to Armageddon the visitors were showboating!

Of course, the Lions put the work in but there was as much inspiration as perspiration. The advice of players was sought and acted upon. There was a pattern but it was a pattern of individuals. If the King wanted to practise his soccer penalty kicks rather than the conventional attempts at goal, then he practised his soccer penalty kicks. But it is no accident that this revolution happened on tour. Under such circumstances, there is time to work on detail and the coach knows that he has a settled party which is not at the whim of selectors from one match to the next. But most, here was a man who understood the game inside out. He put paid to the idea that a coach will necessarily coach flair and imagination out of a player, that all will be played by numbers to the detriment of the game.

When he spoke, aphorisms abound. On forward play: *The first function of a forward is to win possession.* On others cheating: *...not that we wanted to get our retaliation in first.* On the fall away pass: *It is in the finest public school tradition but God, it's useless half the time.* The role of the coach: *He must resolve all that is difficult into something simple.* The counter-attack: *If the opposition are dull enough to kick the ball to you then you must take advantage.* On the old arch enemy, soccer: *It is a good game, it teaches balance, it teaches lots of things. The most important thing it teaches is moving off the ball.* On whether coaches should be excluded from the selection process: *That is mediaeval thinking.* And pre-match training: *It was all related to game situations in Rugby football.*

In short, successful coaching is about knowing the game, attention to detail and being able to select players who can both play and think. Carwyn James felt that, like New Zealand and South Africa, the British could develop their own style. There was no need to ape those previously dominant nations. Wales, in the short term, did well out of it but the Welsh Establishment never trusted James or allowed him to influence the long term. He had to be content with Llanelli and the odd clandestine coffee with the Barbarians. It may not be a coincidence that today, both at club and national level, Welsh rugby is in the doldrums—with the honourable exception of Carwyn's old club.

Of course, there were voices in the North of England who retorted, 'We've been doing this for bloody years' and indeed they had, but old prejudices prevailed and they continued like pelicans in the wilderness to lament their cause. Nevertheless, it did appear that things in England might be improving. John Elders was coach in the 1970s, in which time England beat Australia, New Zealand, South Africa and Wales. In retrospect, this was an astonishing set of results but they were dismissed, as was Elders, as a one-off bit of luck rather than the basis for future development. But it proved two things—that England must be able to produce some pretty decent players and that, on tour, they had the time to develop some sort of coherent game plan that they were unable, for a number of reasons, to achieve at home.

In addition, England Schools had unearthed a rich vein of talent. For example, in 1977, the Under 19 side completed the Grand Slam, which included a 26-0 drubbing of Wales at Cardiff. Again, it was obvious that England had the players to compete at the highest level. Some of these players made their way into the senior set-up. But too many were lost in the morass of club rugby or, fed up with the apparent lack of organisation, threw in their lot with Rugby League. An instance of this general incompetence was when a member of the victorious '77 Schools' side received a communication from the RFU that he was on stand-by for senior international duty. The player in question had, by this stage, been playing Rugby League for some time.

Despite all this, there were the occasional successes. Beaumont's Grand Slam side was born out of a tour to the Far East where plans were hatched, then nurtured, by a sense of injustice. The players knew that it was the system and not themselves that made them the butt of Celtic ridicule and Antipodean disdain. In the main, the team consisted of Northern and Leicester players, a division and club who were used to winning. For a moment, the century-old order was restored. Perhaps if matters had been left in the hands of those who understood the game, who saw it as a contest to be won rather than a prelude to a piss-up, things might have changed. But it was not to be. Committees creaked their way to ineffectual compromise and the English Union settled back to snooze in its usual fur-lined rut.

But in 1984 English rugby had a wake-up call. The Australians, coached by Alan Jones, arrived on these shores. Guided by the ball-handling skills and tactical acumen of their fly half, Mark Ella, they brought a new dimension. Like the Lions of 71 and 74, they were keen to move the ball wide and attack from depth. However, the channel that had opened up for John Williams & Co had long been closed by the drift defence. So the Australians countered by attacking in numbers. A defending wing would find himself having to tackle not only his opposite number but also the whole of the Australian back row. His own back row was nowhere to be seen, either chasing the shadows of dummy runners or outpaced by long and accurate miss passes. Like the rucking New Zealand forwards, the Australian support players took no shortcuts but worked to hit the line at pace and at an angle that would wrongfoot the opposition. The traditional wisdom had been, first drive the ball over the gain line, get the other side on the back foot and then move it wide. Over the years defences had learnt how to negate this manoeuvre and the game was moving towards stalemate. The Australians did not attempt to breach the impenetrable but, through deft ball handling and clever lines of running, simply outflanked the first wave of defence and released support players in numbers. The British game that a decade ago had broken the mould was once again playing catch-up.

In fact, we shouldn't have been taken by surprise. In 1978 the Australian schoolboys had toured England. The squad contained many of the key players who were to return six years later. They were extremely successful with an unprecedented win over England 9-31, this just a year after England Schools had completed the Grand Slam, including the rout of Wales at Cardiff. However, no one took much notice. Schoolboy rugby was very pretty but would not stand up in the real world. Besides, no one took Australian Rugby Union that seriously. Not even the Australians. The proper winter games were Rugby League and Aussie Rules. In footy terms, Union came a long way behind, only just ahead of a semi-contact version played by Italian immigrants.

And they were right. Australian Rugby Union could produce good, or even great, players but not in sufficient numbers to threaten the world order. Rugby Union was strong in the private schools but on leaving the better players would opt for Rugby League where, of course, they could earn money. While on tour in Queensland in 1990, we played a prestigious independent school. There, sport still carried with it all the honours-board and braided-blazer trimmings that the English had abandoned in the sixties. I was, therefore, surprised to learn that the current centres at Brisbane Broncos were former pupils. At the time it was rather like discovering that two Old Etonians were playing in the middle for Wigan.

Clearly something had happened to change the order of things that would allow an also-ran to win the World Cup twice in eight years, in both cases away from home. Those closer to the Australian scene may well know the real truth but from this perspective one thing was very clear. Alan Jones was the innovative coach and either he or someone else had persuaded a significant number of key players of the 1978 squad to stick with Union. The drift towards League had been stemmed. There may have been other reasons. Perhaps the Australian RFU was less concerned about the Yeatsian beast of professionalism that was slouching towards Twickenham. Perhaps someone realised that if they were to become World Champions at everything, it would make sense to split the players between both codes. But it seems to me that the Australian RFU owes a great debt to Alan Jones. Even if I am wrong and the credit lies elsewhere, the game itself should most certainly acknowledge his contribution. Like Carwyn James, Jones showed that with vision–and faith in that vision–you could display all the skill and grace of the dancer without losing the physical confrontation that is an inherent part of the game. Between them, they showed that there was considerably more to Rugby Union than the kick and rush of consenting adults behind the closed doors of middle-class smugness.

A year or four later–a micro-second in terms of RFU forward planning–Geoff Cooke was appointed coach to the national team. He did two things that were unusual. He appointed a young man as captain and he made it harder to be left out of the English team than it was to get into it. This security of tenure, both symbolic and actual, was exactly what the players needed. Cooke created a party on tour playing at home. They had time to formulate a game plan and set a series of targets that were realistically attainable: dominate the Five Nations Championship, perform well in the 1991 World Cup, and then win it in 1995. For the first time, England had a professional side and the man in the street started to notice a game that had previously passed him by.

As an English supporter, you had to approve of Cooke's method but not necessarily admire. England were definitely bullies rather than dancers. The game was played by numbers. Points were accumulated through penalties rather than tries and the spectre of the Murrayfield defeat in 1990 continually hovered. It was the best of times in terms of results but in some ways the worst. The innate conservatism of the Anglo Saxon prevailed and it appeared that nothing had been learnt from the likes of James and Jones. The southern hemisphere continued to dominate and the best that England could offer was a last minute drop goal against a bunch of ageing Aussies. When it really mattered, this group of players played their southern counterparts five times and lost four. If I replay the video of my mind, I can only visualise one try from that period. England are defending in their own 22. Standard procedure: kick the ball out of play deep into the Scottish half and fiercely contest the lineout. But the fly half is not Andrew but Barnes. The pass from the scrum half is sufficiently poor that Barnes has to sidestep to avoid annihilation. Space is created and he accelerates into the gap. Guscott cruises on to his shoulder. Barnes offloads. Half the field is covered before Underwood is given the ball and a certain try. The crucial moment of the move was when the ball missed an inside centre whose instinct was to cut back to the protection of his all powerful pack. Now that was a try to admire. One was left wondering what might have happened if that particular *pas de trois* had been given more rein.

Then, in the niceties of the nineties, another curious thing happened. The behemoth that was the Rugby Football Union did two things. It accepted professionalism, not only among the players but also among the administration, and employed Clive Woodward as coach of the national side. It could be argued that the first was inevitable. If you need to make serious money you don't leave affairs in the hands of a committee and, despite the squeals from the shires, the matter was a done deal. Interestingly, the last bastions of amateurism—or, to be more precise, protectionism—were hoist with their own petard. To sustain the myth of democratic procedure which was at the heart of their argument, they had to accept that the democratically elected leaders knew best. After much spluttering, the opposition retired without so much as a Parthian shot.

The appointment of Woodward was much more significant. Wittingly or unwittingly, the Establishment had employed someone who understood the modern game. He realised that England, with its growing ethnic mix, had the physical and athletic abilities to compete with the best; that there existed a cauldron of players who knew, given a fair chance, they could beat anyone; and that, by combining the various strengths of the regions, he might evolve an English style that could become a world leader. It may be that in the stilly watches of the East India Club reservations were mooted. But it was too late.

Woodward did three things that mattered. First, he undertook the so-called Tour to Hell against Australia, New Zealand and South Africa, not only with dignity but also with vision. He saw that, although without his senior players the side would be heavily defeated, he would, nevertheless, learn a lot about his young players. The fact that we can't envisage

Jonny Wilkinson missing a kick in front of goal is because he did just that on that tour and vowed it would never happen again. In addition, when the RFU put its perceived third-rate team in a third-rate hotel, Woodward moved them to the best in town, on the strength, if necessary, of his own credit card. Second, he would always select long-term footballers over short-term expediency. His coaching credentials had relied on that and he did not bottle his principles. Third, when the players tried to exercise their collective muscle to overcome the intransigence of the RFU, he made it clear that there were greater factors at work than 19th-century trades unionism and that he was not prepared to get involved in a 'them and us situation'. If you didn't want to play, he'd find someone who did. The result is that England now has a group of players who feel secure in the system but know that no one has a place as of right. How it will turn out is to be seen but there is no doubt that Woodward has already done for England and rugby what James and Jones did for their respective countries and the game at large. Let us hope, this time round, the greater picture is considered.

7

Warms-Up I Have Missed and Other Confessions of an England Selector

The highly successful coaches of Chapter Six were dealing with a more or less finished product. Their job was to put their preconceived plan into practice and, more importantly, persuade the players to act in accordance. I am sure they would be the first to acknowledge all the work put in from the earliest of ages at schools, clubs and through the various representative sides that made this end product possible. With the exception of New Zealand, South Africa and, from time to time, various areas of Wales, Rugby Union has traditionally come a poor second in the world of winter field sports. It owes much to these enthusiasts and volunteers that the current Rugby World Cup ranks only after Football and the Olympics as an international event.

So what do these enthusiasts contribute? Or, more accurately, what is their objective? In mission-speak it would be something like 'to identify and develop talented young rugby players so that they can perform with credit on the appropriate representative stage'. What has emerged from a far less precise way of thinking is that the selector/coach follows a more or less similar pathway. The best young players are identified, their skills are developed and representative matches are arranged. Often these three objectives merge and confuse each other but I feel that the English rugby world should examine each stage separately and carefully to ensure each element is equally catered for.

It is probably best to examine the last item first for, as has often been pointed out, 'in our ends are our beginnings', and ask, should there be representative rugby at youth level at all? Those who are against it, or at least an excess of it, can put a valid case. They would argue that the need to win the immediate game takes precedence over player development, that time is spent on drills rather than individual skills and that selection and coaching sessions are skewed to ensure the maximum exploitation of the disposable talent. They would accept that there should be matches but very much on a festival basis, with sufficient flexibility of substitution that it would be pointless trying to decide whether anyone had won or lost. If the real motive lying behind the organisation of

Youth rugby is to invest every player with the maximum opportunity to develop and fully participate, then the case is difficult to refute.

But there is also a real world that demands success and this is inhabited as much by players as patriots. The ultimate point of a game is that it has a definite outcome. Even a draw can be seen as a success or failure. To have an outcome, you have to have a match and, as the name suggests, this means pitting one group against another. The groups may be arbitrary but they have to have an exclusive identity. As a result, in English rugby there exist school, club, district, county, divisional and national sides. This group identity means a great deal to a good number of people and it is this sort of person who tends to play and support team games. They relish the tribal identity and believe it gives shape and purpose to the exercise. It is an interesting aside that when educational philosophy swung away from team games in favour of individual achievement, the move coincided with the rise of football hooliganism amongst the young. Most adolescents will abide by rules if they see that they make sense or become a condition of entry into the chosen activity. But, as William Golding so presciently pointed out in *The Lord of the Flies,* if you remove the infrastructure, they will soon make rules for themselves. I suspect that if there were matches with no significant outcome, young players would soon lose interest and find an alternative that had a satisfactory, if not necessarily salutary, result.

Of all team games, rugby seems more than most to require that sense of identity. You are not going to put your head where it hurts unless you are concerned about the collective outcome. The side that is the less willing to commit itself will almost certainly lose. There has to be an inner commitment to winning, coupled with a belief that if you strive sufficiently you will prevail. In addition, the game is constructed in such a way that, no matter the nature of their role, all can feel that they have been meaningfully involved and equally deserving of the laurels. The only way a group of players can become such a team is by playing together on a regular basis in a series of matches that matter. This means that in the scheme of Youth rugby there has to be a sufficient number of representative matches.

As both sides have a sustainable argument, then a sensible compromise needs to be found. As the most common form of representative rugby is at school or club, it is probably best to examine the position first at this level. You could argue that playing every week is excessive and that the necessary match preparations eat into time that should be spent on player development. But one of the clubs' main worries is that if they do not offer a programme of regular fixtures, players tend to drift into other activities. Also, many independent schools see sporting prowess as an important factor in the market place and want to play (and beat) as many of their competitors as possible. A solution might be that clubs and schools should rethink the traditional structure of inter-age matches. The 'fixture' might take place over two weekends, one as a joint development session and the other the match proper. This might be particularly attractive to schools where rugby is a secondary or emerging sport and who currently avoid fixtures where they will be little more than cannon-fodder. It might also persuade clubs to move their youth programme to a Saturday and thus be forced to spread their net outside the rugby-playing schools in their area.

Above this strata of representative rugby there are four further levels: District, County, Divisional and National. Practice varies around the country but generally District sides are at Under 15 and below and act as a preparation for the County side at 16, and the

Divisional side is a selectorial tool in the National process. If the superior sides were abolished, the lesser would either disappear or take their place. So, in real terms, it is only necessary to examine the need and value of County and National sides.

The case for the continuation of County sides is very strong. Players with ability must have the opportunity to play at a level where they can develop their skills and understanding of the game in the company of players of similar ability. The surest way to retard development is for the player to allow himself to play in the comfort zone. If he operates as the big fish in the small pond, as he might otherwise have to, there is little chance that he will keep pace with his peers who are continually put under pressure. It could be argued that the same effect could be achieved by dividing the countries into a number of equally rugby-populated regions but to do so would mean abandoning the existing County structure and, as a result, lose an important strand of the community game. No matter how high the youthful aspiration, only a few will make it to the top. Playing County rugby will be the pinnacle for many very good players and gives pleasure to players, schools and clubs alike. Players who fail to reach the élite apex must not, as they do in soccer, feel that they are rejects but an important and contributary part of the pyramid. County matches are embedded in the history of the game and history is the mortar of any civilised institution. It would be a brave man who decided to abolish a Roses match, at any level, on the grounds that it was little more than a selectorial exercise.

The case for a side or sides to be selected to play at international level is less secure. It has to happen sometime. If the first opportunity a player has of meeting an All Black is in the qualifying rounds of a World Cup, both he and his side will be under a severe disadvantage. The question is when the process of familiarising the player with the international arena should begin. It must not be so soon that the wrong group of players are exposed to the experience or so late that there is little opportunity to learn from the process. On one hand, it would be a waste of money and time if an early programme concentrated on a squad of players who were only the best because of premature physical development. On the other, if left too late, the scars of failure may have too little time to heal. What is certain is that there is a need for a co-ordinated plan where players reach a particular plateau of experience at each particular stage. For example, at 16, the emphasis could be on proper pre-match preparation, with all that that involves. It must be remembered that at this age there will be players who have never, independently, spent time away from home. You can be as homesick in Surrey as in Sydney. What is more, they should play in a major stadium before as big a crowd as can be mustered. At 18/19, the players could be involved in an overseas tour so they can experience the reality of living in a party for a number of weeks. At 21, they could take part in an international tournament with all the pressures that such a competition entails.

It is generally agreed that 16 is the very earliest that merits such an investment and it would probably be wise if the programme at this level is not over-ambitious in playing terms. The current arrangement whereby the 16 Group play Italy and Wales seems more than adequate. However, there are those who feel that even 16 is too early and that, at this age, four Divisional sides playing festival rugby is the prudent way forward. They would argue that from these squads would emerge an on-going élite development programme that would culminate in an Under 19 team. They would leave the identification of the better players in each Division to professional co-ordinators supported by volunteers from the clubs and schools. Players would be added to or discharged from the squads as the years pass but the ultimate outcome would be to select a group which could be nurtured to perform successfully at senior level.

This looks a good idea on paper but has two serious drawbacks. The first is that the volunteers may quickly lose interest if they feel they are being excluded from the decision-making process and merely used to fetch and carry. This would be especially true if it were felt that the professionals were not doing as good a job as the amateurs had done in the past. Such a judgment would not only relate to their success in identifying and developing the player but also to the welfare of the child in general educational terms. Would, for example, an employee of the RFU, whose job specification, either explicitly or implicitly, demands that he produces a requisite number of top players in a given time, be more concerned with training schedules of his own choosing or dovetailing his demands into a programme for exam revision? Moreover, volunteers need to feel that they are valued, and putting together an International side is often seen as the cherry on the cake.

The second drawback is that the number of players originally chosen to make up the Divisional squads will be dramatically pruned. Of the original 120 players whose expectations have been raised at 16, cost may demand that little more than twenty would be required to feed the élite system in three years time. So what would happen to the remaining 100? There would, no doubt, be assurances that if there was sufficient evidence of development they would invited to return to the fold, and much talk of 'parachuting' a discarded player back into the community game. But this should fool no one. If you miss the cut you are going to play catch-up in terms of development, and this at an age when the learning curve is at its most exponential. Experience has shown that players at this age who look first choice and then miss crucial development through, say, injury, return several rungs down the ladder. This can happen in as little as three weeks, let alone three years.

Any idea that the player and his parents, who are still to a large extent controlling his destiny, will accept this with equanimity is optimistic in the extreme. Much will have been made about pathways and rungs of the ladder to international glory and to be unceremoniously dumped (with or without parachute) is understandably disconcerting for boys at this stage of their emotional development. If the representatives of the RFU are to take over the pastoral role, they might be in for a shock when they face the fury of a parent scorned. It would make sense and engender important goodwill if the system started at 16 was mirrored, albeit in a streamlined form, up to the moment when most rugby players leave school and would therefore be able to continue to participate in the process of Divisional and representative rugby that is currently in place. At 18, they are deemed capable of making their own decisions and are far better placed to do so—with or without the hell-hath-no-furies. If players, for whatever reason, have to leave school but still wish seriously to pursue a career in rugby, they could be attached to a senior club or other suitable 'educational provider' who would submit their nominations for youth trials as if they were still at school. A final but not insignificant fact is that many individual schools are already unhappy about losing players to representative rugby at the expense of their own results. They see there is some point if they can boast of International Caps in the prospectus. 'Attended Active Sports Training Session' does not have quite the same ring.

The nature of the Under 18 side or sides could be re-examined and a suggestion might be that there is a 1st September side which plays incoming tourists at Christmas and a 1st January side which plays the Home Nations at Easter. This programme would culminate in an overseas tour once the exam period was over. It would be important that the players selected to make such a tour were contractually committed to playing professional rugby and that the tour was seen as the beginning of a course which they followed to the point of graduation, with the Under 21 Cup Squad as their 'degree' award.

If this amount of control were retained by those who run the Schools' Union, it would be imperative that they did not live in an ivory tower of their own making. They should strive to be as socially inclusive as possible and not rely on the well turned-out independent schoolboy. They should also be accountable to the Rugby Union and gear their selection and development programmes to the national guidelines and actively seek advice from others outside the educational system. There are those who will claim that in the brave new world of professionalism a new broom would sweep away the weaknesses of the past. A reasonable counter to that argument might be that, of the players whom Clive Woodward chose to put together in an unprecedented run of unbeaten matches against the best sides in the world, 24 had been identified and, to a significant extent, developed by the Schools' Union.

If I have given the question of representative rugby an exhaustive (some may say exhausting) airing, it is because I believe that the objectives and outcomes should be chosen before any programme of selection and development is put into place. Too often the opposite has tended to be true. Squads are formed and then people decide what is to be done with them. How many clubs have announced a Youth policy for 18s to 21s without any fixtures in place? How often have such schemes folded?

The identification of talented players begins at school or club. It is extremely unlikely that a player who has the ability to become a national star would be overlooked at this level. It would therefore be tempting to ignore this stage of the process and move up the selectorial ladder to examine the success or otherwise of the present system at a regionally-based level. This might be a mistake. If the school or club has limited resources of talent, there is a temptation to position such a player as near to the ball as possible. It is therefore not unlikely that a future international prop might well start his career in the back row and that all gifted footballers are selected at fly half. Players of this age are suspicious of moving position, preferring the devil they know, and consequently at later stages of selection there can be a log jam of numbers 8 and 10. As a result, the system has to be pretty sophisticated if good players are not to be missed. I can remember, some decades ago, a County trial where we had to choose between thirteen good to goodish fly halves without a decent three-quarter in sight. We sorted something out but it all ended in tears, with a large and vigorous Lancashire back row trampling all over a somewhat frail inside centre whose previous concept of defence had been to leave it to others. It is not only players who prefer to go with the devil. There is often as much reluctance on the part of coaches to give individuals the opportunity to change the number on their shirt, if it means undermining a proven game-plan.

Given that each County finds all the best players available in its area, there are still difficulties. The Divisional selectors will watch the best players from each County but does that mean they are watching the best players available? In the North of England,

Yorkshire have 180 schools affiliated to the County Union, Cumbria has 37. It only takes a moment's thought to realise that a Yorkshire 2nd XV might be more than a match for Cumbria's best side. There are further problems. In a large county there may easily be two talented players challenging for the same position on the representative side. Some positions in the squad will double up, scrum half for example, and the selectors, if they were doing their job properly, would make sure they assessed the understudy of any outstanding player. But suppose the position in question is full back. It is unlikely that the county would carry the second choice full back amongst its replacements. The apparent also-ran disappears from the selection process, yet may well be the second best player in that position in the whole country. The other side of the coin is the talented winger who is playing in a weak side. It is not impossible that he may never have a real chance to show his paces. On top of this, counties want to win their matches and coaches organise sides so that strengths are exploited and weaknesses hidden. The most damaging example of this is the selection of a burly but otherwise unexceptional player to carry the ball up at inside centre, who then does so regardless of the opportunities and players around him.

Clearly a selection system that relies on watching county matches alone is seriously flawed as it will almost certainly end up losing, perhaps for ever, players of quality. The Divisions have tried to address this problem by having an interim development weekend before the Final Trial. They invite not only the players who have clearly made their mark in the County games but also any other players who appear to have potential but have failed for one reason or another to show it. This group includes the starved winger, the hidden full back and anyone of County standard who is returning from injury. In particular, it gives a second chance to the player from a limited Rugby Union background who at this stage comes second to a player who is more accomplished but not necessarily of greater potential. Over a weekend it is possible to arrange a variety of circumstance that allows a fuller judgment to be made, both as to a player's ability and which position might suit him best.

This compromise of proper assessment whilst maintaining the County programme has worked well. Players who do not make the Divisional squad at 16 can still be made to feel part of an ongoing system and encouraged to learn from the experience and try again in the future. One such example is James Simpson-Daniel. He joined the North of England Development weekend as a 16 year-old fly half. He had talent, but in the opinion of the selectors and coaches did not merit a place in the Final Trial. As he himself later admitted, he did not have sufficient confidence in his own ability at that stage of his development. Things changed, his confidence grew and he gave it a go. As a result he was picked for the Under 18 side in the centre and, a year or so after leaving school, the full England squad as a wing.

If this were the norm, it would be a complete vindication of a system that maintains the ethos of the County system whilst ensuring equal opportunity for all. But such a view would be too complacent and self-satisfied. Simpson-Daniel had two things in his favour, either of which could have ensured this success. First, he attended a rugby playing school of some repute and, second, his elder brother had already played for England Schools. Either of these advantages ensured that if there was any evidence of improvement both he and his family knew how to get back on board. But what would have happened if it had been Jim Smith who, having attended an 11–

16 state school which played rugby and had supported his cause, now attended a Sixth Form College that did neither. He would not have done enough at 16 to have independent schools dangling the carrots of rugby scholarships or senior clubs queuing for his signature to join their academy. Perhaps for every Simpson-Daniel saved, there are a dozen or so lost.

All this seems to add weight to those who wish to abolish the Schools' Union and the part it plays in identifying and developing players for the future, and replace it with a centrally-controlled group of professionals. Indeed, it does and if the ERFSU is to continue to participate in the process, it would be foolish to ignore the flaws or paper over the cracks. Instead, it should present its own case that properly compares with the suggestions made by the Rugby Football Union's Review of Schools, Students & Youth Rugby. This suggests a division of the country into regions of roughly equal playing strength and setting up, monitoring and controlling age-group squads of players aged 14–18 who would form the basis for representative rugby and a reservoir that would channel the very best players into an élite system based on fourteen National Academies. In this way, the most talented players would be fast-tracked to reach the standards set by Youth rugby in the southern hemisphere and the remainder enthused with the game until, as adults, they are filtered into community rugby at large.

Put like this, it seems the best possible solution—an unending stream of talent to rule the world and a bottomless pit of enthusiasts to play, referee, coach and administer the game. But is the best solution possible? Is there any danger that the plug might be pulled? There are three potential plug holes, the disappearance down any of which would seriously undermine the proposals put forward in the Review, and a combination of all three could destroy the policy before it has the chance to implement itself.

The first of these is the disappearance of the volunteer. The Review accepts that the support of such individuals is essential to the success of the scheme and bases its general recommendations on that assumption. There is much talk of valuing the volunteer but little substance as to how that is going to happen. In any consideration it would be sensible to examine the salient points. First, what is the nature of these volunteers? Why do they start? Why do they stay? They may start for a variety of reasons, from a wish to serve the community to a desire to jump on

the bandwagon. They stay because they hope for some reward or because they feel under an obligation. It is the second of these motives that is of interest and should be addressed. A sense of obligation is the result of a recognition of a responsibility, a feeling that if you don't carry on with something of your own making then the project will suffer. Once others are appointed over your head, then the sense of obligation can disappear, particularly if the newcomer is being paid to do the job that you had previously performed gratis!

If the schoolteachers who have supported the youth side of the game for so long decided that their implicit educational responsibilities had ended, the cost of replacing that manpower would be prohibitive. In the front of the ERFSU handbook are listed the volunteers who administer the Union and select, manage and coach the International sides at 16 and 18. This numbers 127 separate posts. Below this level are the four Divisions, each of which has officers, selectors and management and coaching teams which would number, at a minimum, 25 for each Division and, feeding them, 28 County Schools' Unions with a similar minimum number of key workers. In other words, at the various AGMs around the country the best part of 1000 posts are annually filled by unpaid labour to run Youth rugby. Of course, these posts vary in the amount of time it takes to fulfil the required responsibilities, but let us assume the average, including travelling time, is two hours a week (I can hear the snorts of derision as I type this). Even at the modest level of pay that is a legal minimum wage, it would mean an expenditure that would exceed the monies currently being spent by the RFU on Schools' and Youth rugby. It is not surprising that the Union refers to this arrangement as a partnership. It is to be hoped that one of the partners doesn't decide to sleep.

The second imponderable is the part that the independent schools will choose to play. There is an uncomfortably close parallel between such institutions and the Premier Clubs. Both have commercial agendas that do not always conform with the wishes of the RFU. In the case of the Clubs, the Union can wield the financial stick but it has no such control over the independent sector of education. Headteachers may decide, for a variety of reasons, that they do not wish their pupils to enter into the RFU's plans–which decision, as matters stand, would create a considerable gap in the programme. In time, the RFU could doubtless produce a side that did not rely on the rugby played at private schools and draw its stars from the public sector. The Oxbridge colleges have also espoused such a scheme but, to date, even the most liberal of dons has found it quicker said than done.

Third, there is the matter of venue and timing. Rugby has traditionally been part of a school's extra-curricular activities, taking place after school and at weekends. If travel was necessary, it was arranged by the school and the pupil was put to the minimum of inconvenience. Latterly, the local club has taken on a similar role and acted in a like manner. If the RFU had to rely on employing professionals to take over the role of development and player identification, would it be able to attract suitable employees whose working hours are essentially evenings and weekends? Teachers have accepted these unsociable hours in return for lengthy holidays at other times. I am not so sure it would have happened if the normal contract had been a 48-week working year.

Finally, we come to development and also the title of the chapter. In my days as a national selector, the Chairman would insist that, once a squad had been selected, we all attended training sessions, not to offer advice but as an act of solidarity with the coaching staff. Inevitably, the sessions would start with the necessary warm-up. This, as often as not, involved the use of the Antipodean Grid in which four queues, in the form of a cross, play a combined version of pass the parcel and musical chairs. This has many merits. It is simple to arrange, requires little imagination to organise and is high on work ethic. Above all, it appears to have a sense of purposeful activity. But, as Carwyn James said of the Lions tour in New Zealand:

I seem to recall that down in Wanganui for instance, we had a training session there and the locals were not terribly impressed, and then the local side had a training session a couple of hours after and they really worked hard apparently, running, running, running, and they all thought it was a most impressive session. It depends on how you look at them. It comes back to the point, of the physical nature of the game where people very often are unthinking and are also unsmiling [...] I think it is important to see the game in perspective. John Williams said once that there should always be a moment in the game when a person can smile at something. We had the impression of unsmiling giants, a machine geared to play a certain way. That's why I felt it was so important for our boys to be thinking at all times. You've got to out-think the opposition. You've got to think for yourself.

I would watch the players performing in the grids. Once the pattern had been established, eyes would start to glaze over. Virtually all had done a similar exercise countless times before at countless other training sessions. I found it rather depressing. Here is a young man about to embark on the sporting moment of his dreams and the best that could be offered in the way of introduction was running by rote. Of course, much that followed was of the highest standard in terms of player development but I felt that really the affair had got off on the wrong foot. My theory is that if you are going to sell a game to the young you must make all aspects of preparation and playing as interesting and intriguing as possible. In the hands of a person whose livelihood may well depend on the outcome, there has to be a danger that the fun will go. So, if the occasion offered, I would miss this particular part of the proceedings and conduct my own version of the warm-up in the clubhouse until I saw something happening on the field that appeared to relate to the actual game itself.

8

In League with the Devil?

In the middle of the last decade of the last century, the international ruling body of Rugby Union pronounced the game open. Even then it seemed that, like Macbeth's 'Amen', the word 'professional' stuck in the throat. As in tennis and golf before it, a euphemism had to do. But euphemism or no, open meant professional and professional meant what it said—that players who could generate cash by persuading the public to pay to watch them perform wanted a sizeable portion of the gates receipts. One immediate (certainly in rugbytime) reaction was that the RFU realised that it would have to adopt an equally professional approach to the making of significant commercial decisions, rather than allowing them to lurch from one committee meeting to the next. To that end, it, or we, or whoever owned the game at that time, appointed a chief executive who, true to form, knocked 10% off all budgets, sacked existing members of staff and developed the necessary apparatus to make important and pressing decisions. This was A Good Thing and allowed the erstwhile beached whale to be refloated into the waters of fiscal realism. The outcome was impressive. The considerable cost of refurbishing Twickenham was repaid and a financial agreement with the Premier Clubs was established. The equation, in corporate terms, was simple. To run the game you need money; to make money you need full houses and competitive TV bids; to get full houses, etc, you need a very successful England team; to get such a team you need money.

Clearly, the nature of this equation means that if any link fails, the entire system collapses. But Francis Baron had inherited a fortunate moment in time. English rugby had a generous number of talented players and, in Clive Woodward, a coach who was his own man and prepared to risk failure to achieve eventual success. Success in the 2003 World Cup was the medium target, with world domination the long-term aim. So, was everything in place to achieve this ambition? The players for the future were there, as they had always been. All that was needed was to develop a structure that identified and developed them. But the income stream was not necessarily as secure. The people who, for the most part, watched

Rugby Union in England were rugby players past and present who belonged to a particularly affluent economic group. If they lost interest, so would commercial television. It was therefore essential that rugby and an interest in rugby continued to thrive at its traditional grass roots level. The solution was once again to divide the game into two halves. An Elite Group, controlled by the Performance Department, to provide the players, and a Programme of Community Rugby that would support and expand the game and provide the audience. It was, and is, an important balancing act. At best, talented players could be seduced from the traditionally successful sports and the support base broadened. At worst, ruggermania might rise to soccer's xenophobic patriotism, or whoever plays Lady Macbeth to Satellite TV might develop a penchant for hockey.

Thus came about the review of Youth rugby that laid out the plans for an élite performance programme from the cradle to the sporting grave. The main plank of its platform was the foundation of a number of Academies for the 16–21 age group, which were to be situated at strategic regional points and coincided, for practical purposes, with the existence of a Premier Club which had suitable facilities. The chosen

165

player would be attached to the appropriate Academy, to which he would log on as he would to the Internet. He would continue his normal educational and playing process and the Academy would come to him in the form of his mentor. From time to time he would be called to headquarters for additional polishing. The advantages of such a scheme are obvious. There would be minimal disruption of normal life. Experts would be on hand to monitor such matters as fitness, training and diet appropriate to the individual and the RFU would have a clearly identified source of players who contractually had committed themselves to playing rugby as a career.

In practice, it may not be so straightforward. By the time the RFU had launched its idea of an Academy, the Premier Clubs were well under way with academies of their own. The two sound the same (the upper or lower case is difficult to distinguish in conversation) but in fact they are very different in concept. The RFU Academy sees its protégés as individuals who may, in the long term, become part of the English senior side. They belong, as it were, to Club England. A Premier Club will see its academy as a supply line for its senior team. The two have different agendas. It would not matter to the RFU if all its chosen élite at one particular club were props, provided the other positions were located elsewhere. Whereas the Club's academy would have to cater for the full range of positions as part of its future planning. The RFU would not see its Academy players being part of a side; in fact, they might get all their playing experience outside the Premier Club itself. The Club on the other hand would, in all probability, want to run an academy XV and wish to imbue the coaching policy the Club espoused. The problem is that the Joe Bloggs of Club England could also be joebloggs@premclub.com and that he could be torn in a variety of directions. If this seems confusing to the reader, it must be disconcerting to a 16 year-old who is trying to decide on his future.

Of course, if the development plans of the RFU and the Club are completely dovetailed, then all problems could probably be dealt with on a one-by-one basis. But conflict is likely. Let us take one simple example. Joe is a talented 19 year-old fly half but not an especially good place kicker. The RFU, to whom he is contracted, wants him to play in the Premier Club's First XV to gain valuable experience. The Club, on the other hand, is trying to dig itself out of the relegation zone and, for very obvious reasons, wants to play an experienced South African ex-international who can kick penalties from his own half. Something has to give and it may well be the poor old or, in this case, young pig in the middle.

Even if the juggling act is successfully managed, it does not mean that the outcome will be equally successful. Before the England match against Wales last season *The Guardian* ran an article under the banner 'A nation strains to find answers to a lost chord', in which, following the defeat against Italy, a Welsh think-tank was asked to consider what had prompted the decline and whether there were signs of recovery. John Scott, formerly of Cardiff and England, had this to say:

> *I think there is a problem with the younger generation. My son Liam, born and brought up in Wales, is 15 and nearly 6ft 4in. He plays soccer on a Saturday and rugby on a Sunday. One of his mates is in the Wales Under-16 [rugby] side and spends all week training. The kid looks worn out. Liam and his pals look at him and see no point in going down that road. The fun has to be put back.*

And one of the main elements of fun in a team game is that it is a team game and pleasure is taken from the camaraderie that goes with it. An Academy player may well become isolated from this environment. If it is decided that for the sake of his own development he has to miss school matches or steps on the representative ladder, will he feel that he is missing out on the 'fun'? Will team coaches welcome the return of the diva and be comfortable with ditching a player who has so willingly contributed in the great man's absence, or be happy to change their team plan to accommodate some greater design? In fact, will the whole concept of élitism be so alien to the sense of the game that the run-of-the-mill player previously attracted by its egalitarian opportunities will lose interest and see yet again that sport means not social recreation but a business opportunity for the talented few? Finally, does the Academy route really suit the English psyche? There is no doubting the success of the system in Australia, which has produced outstanding results in all sports (I think only curling has escaped the net), but does it mean their success will be replicated over here? Playing catch-up is never a very good idea and any Performance Director has to look hard into the very heart and soul of the game at hand rather than coming up with a plan that has been successful elsewhere. The questions in this paragraph all add up to the really important one that should be

169

addressed. It is not *Why did they beat us?* but *How can we beat them?*

Moreover, fun does not necessarily mean frivolity. There can be as much pleasure in solving a problem that interests you as indulging in simply hedonistic activities. I am sure that Liam's mate would have felt less 'worn out' if he had looked forward to training with the expectation of novelty rather than repetition. Defence strategy is now the rage and the gospel according to St Phil holds sway. Like the grid, it is easy to organise, involves any number of people and looks impressively active. But pressuring the attacking player in your zone in the knowledge that the colleagues next to you are guarding against the inside or outside break is scarcely rocket science and has had to be mastered quite quickly by any schoolboy team that has played sevens seriously. Of course it is important and is the cornerstone of success in today's current beef-fest but, though spending a whole training session trotting backwards and forwards whilst fanning left and right might be perfectly acceptable to the professional adult, it is hardly a bundle of fun for a 15 year-old. It would be a great pity if 'grown-up' rugby is introduced to the young élite player as a muddy variant of formation dancing.

What is considerably more important in, particularly, the formative stage of a player's development, is to concentrate on the individual enhancement of his various playing skills. This falls into three separate areas: physical prowess, mental determination and game understanding. The more a player has of each of these, the better he is. Each sport will have different emphases but the principle is the same, whether you're climbing the North Face of the Eiger, opening the batting at Lords or receiving a try-scoring pass at the moment of apparent personal demolition. That is, with sufficient confidence in your own abilities and proper appreciation of the situation you are in, you are less likely to be panicked into taking a course of action that could well prove irreversible.

Of the three areas, I would consider the last to be the one to concentrate on at this moment in a young player's rugby life. Of the other two, over-developing the growing body as if it were adult could be a major mistake. Secondly, mental determination is part of the great nature *v* nurture debate. Either you have it genetically or you live in a culture that encourages and approves of the concept of the fight against the odds. In the end, you can do nothing about the former and the latter requires some form of team identification that may not be available at this point of the player's career. To engineer it may not be a good thing as it tends more to the said formation dancing than to formative learning. So, if the coach is most effectively to help the youngster, he must encourage the development of his understanding of the game, or, as the Australians would have it, make him 'rugby-smart'.

There is no doubt that experience is the only way to achieve this and the more intense the experience the better the result. But the nature of the experience must match the point of maturation. Adolescents will become bored with childish games that they have left behind or adult activities which they have yet to appreciate. Different skills are achieved at different stages. Learning how to check a player before evading his grasp is best learned not in the rugby field, where the opportunity might occur only rarely, but in the playground as part of a game of tag. In the same way balance is learnt from climbing trees, and improving hand-eye co-ordination by throwing stones at disused factory windows (or, if you want to increase rather than improve your vocabulary, at passing bargees). Adolescents like games. They take a pleasure in the structure that has been placed on their previous anarchic activities. Throwing missiles at each other becomes cricket, kicking teddy, football. And, once interested, they will continue this process from dawn to dusk. It may be that in Wales the process has been artificially accelerated. Liam's mate, I suspect, was not so much 'worn out' as 'worn down'.

The other problem with developing game-related skills in England is the weather. Assuming that rugby is going to take place in the winter months, it will spend a good deal of its playing time in the wet and cold. Ironically, if the sun does shine, it probably means that the ground is frozen and so too hard to play on. There is nothing we can do about this when we play the game as a match, but to train in such conditions is ludicrous. The Dutch, during the course of revolutionising the game of Association Football, decided that all games played by youngsters should be indoors and six-a-side, thus ensuring maximum ball contact and perfect conditions. The reasons were obvious and the outcome, in terms of skill at adult level, unquestionable. The difficulty is to recreate these benefits in a rugby context. The game needs considerable space in all directions and a soft surface. If the average indoor space available is a basketball court, we seem to be back to Charterhouse.

But basketball is possibly the key. It has the same

ball-handling properties as rugby and if an oval ball is substituted and the goals are vertically-suspended hoops with the centre at waist level, it is not too hard to create a game that contains a reasonable reflection of the handling and passing skills of rugby. Given that you have accepted the move away from the public-school invented rules, you can use these sessions to develop the one attribute that is most difficult of all to coach: decision making. It is even difficult to explain the term in a meaningful manner. When I was selecting, we used to talk to the players before any game in which they were going to be assessed and explain what we, as selectors, were looking for. When it came to decision making, I tried to make it as simple as possible: *Ask yourself the question, 'After I have had the ball in my possession, are my side better or worse off as a result?'* If the answer is usually 'better' rather than 'worse', you are probably making the right decisions.

Again, it's a question of practice. If we go back to the basketball court, it is possible to sharpen a player's response to spur-of-the-moment situations. The game could start by being played under basketball rules but at an arranged signal immediately change to the rules of soccer. The goal would be scored by passing the ball through the hoop under the first circumstance and kicking it through under the second. It would be interesting to see who first works out the value of the drop kick at the moment the rules change. Matters could be made more complex by, on another signal, the sides immediately starting to play as if they had changed ends. The ability to turn defence immediately into attack is often the sign of a good player. An interesting variant is where there are particular rules, such as only X can score or only Y and Z can pass forward, which one side knows and the other doesn't. In this way, skills can be put under mental pressure and players have to develop strategies to deal with the unforeseen. Not all of this will carry over into the full-blown game but, in my experience, these exercises are more likely to attract and entertain the nimble football brain than an endless round of trying to destroy tackle shields.

Much has been made of the lack of flair shown by English sides and with some justification. There is an innate conservatism that pervades sport in this country and, whilst the qualities of grace and steadfast courage are approved, flair and invention have traditionally had a less salubrious reputation. It seemed to smack of dishonesty and fitted into the caricature of a rather dubious Johnny Foreigner–the sort of chap who would sell a dummy is the sort of man who'd shoot a fox type of attitude. As a result, there has been a tendency to select the player who is sound under fire rather than gifted but occasionally wayward. There seem to me to be two reasons for this. First, the Anglo-Saxon as a type is not especially agile, not as gifted in terms of movement and balance as the Celt for example, and so there has been an inclination to develop a game that suited his strengths rather than exposed his weaknesses. Second, too many games are played on a must-win basis, where a costly mistake will be reviled and the cry of *Get it in touch!* is the solution to every defensive dilemma

The first problem could resolve itself. The ethnic mix of Britain is such that the English game is no longer stocked only by those who attended public boarding schools and have surnames preceded by three initials. If the game becomes socially inclusive, which is currently the avowed intention of the RFU, the problem will disappear very quickly. The second is more problematic. Playing safe has become an English mindset and if newcomers to the game are to be berated because they take risks, they may well look elsewhere or, worse, be sucked into the mediocrity that is often the result of over-caution. So the English management made a very sensible decision and that was to take seriously the international sevens circuit. Sevens to many is regarded as irrelevant to the larger game, an end-of-season frolic, but there is no doubt that it acts as an excellent introduction to the talented novice. All the significant attacking and defending skills are being constantly tested without the clutter of time-consuming set pieces.

In addition, the fact that the New Zealanders take it very seriously is testimony to its worth. They probably see it, amongst other things, as a training ground for players of South Sea Island derivation to be imbued with the All Black ethic. For the English, it is an ideal opportunity to develop an alternative outlook among the up-and-coming élite and act as a bridge for Rugby League converts who have decided to change codes. Most importantly, it allows the new wave to play in a prestigious and meaningful international competition that is not constantly under the potentially corrosive microscope of media scrutiny. Schools have taken the smaller game seriously for several decades, seeing it as an opportunity for their more talented players to develop their skills. If it is felt that the Schools are now failing to develop players at a sufficient pace, then perhaps the RFU should consider supporting existing youth national sevens competitions such as Oxford and Rosslyn Park, setting up competitions of its own and raising the profile by playing the semis and finals at Twickenham before international matches.

If we assume that the identification and development of young talent has been satisfactorily organised, does that mean that the rest of the game will run smoothly? Again, there seem to be two main problem areas. Given that you can only play so much golf, how do players occupy their time in a wall-to-wall rugby environment? (I fully appreciate that pre-match preparation and post-match recuperation, with their attention to diet, fitness regimes, thermal sequencing and, for all I know, aromatherapy and transcendental meditation, take time but there still must be the odd chronomatic corner to fill.) And–can the game financially sustain the significant number of professionals who have committed themselves to it?

In answer to the first, I feel that the professional player should feel a responsibility to the game as a whole. He is lucky enough to do something for a

living which he would do for pleasure and should as a quid pro quo give something back to the game that put him in this fortunate position. This could be done by making it a contractual obligation for every player, for example, to take responsibility for a team of 14 year-olds in the club's catchment area. This would not be merely a token visit but the coat-off, blowing-up-balls, ringing-round-for-a-last-minute-re-placement end of the spectrum. The team, Wilko's Wonders, or whatever, would identify with the player, pay to watch him play, develop an identity with the club in question and generally swell the ranks of the rugby community. In return, the player would learn a variety of life skills and develop any talent he might have for coaching after his playing career is over. Players already visit schools and clubs for coaching sessions but this suggestion would need a far greater commitment than running the lads through a few tackling practices and having a beer with the staff afterwards. Perhaps there might even be a league.

An entirely different commitment would be a de-termination to enlarge the playing skills of the game itself. As mentioned, rugby, given the odd shape of a slippery ball, was understandably cautious in its ap-proach. Perhaps now, given time and a sticky ball on his hands, is the moment for the professional player to experiment. The problem facing all attack coaches is how to break down the adamantine defences being thrown up before them. The general view is that there are three ways–through, round or over the top. As the first two have been effectively blocked off, a re-visit to the kick and chase might bear scrutiny. The shape of the ball with its irregular bounce seems to mitigate against the soccer equivalent of turning the defence by sliding the ball inside the full back. But this very uncertainty of bounce could act in the attackers' favour if they knew which way it was going to move. A rugby ball on bouncing can travel in a combination of directions which include forwards, backwards, left and right. If a player could master a kicking technique that produced this variety of movement in a controlled way, the legal forward pass would come into existence.

If the reader doubts the possibility of attaining this level of skill, I can only say that I have witnessed something like it on at least two occasions. Admittedly both were in a coaching situation rather than on the field of play but each was equally impressive. The first, by one of the great wingers of the game, was a demonstration of chipping the ball over the defending opponent, then collecting it at full speed after the first bounce. To make this possible, he had to ensure that on landing the ball stood up rather than continuing its forward momentum. In addition, he could more often than not make it bounce, not only backwards but also towards either his left or right hand to enable him the more easily to step inside or outside the cover. The second exhibition was more informal and inside a large hall. The coaching point being made was that a kicker should have such control that if he kicked a rugby ball against a hard surface he would know the exact angle at which it would return. To illustrate, the player kicked the ball vertically above his head. It hit the ceiling some twenty feet above and, without him moving an inch, descended directly back into his hands. What made the demonstration particularly effective was that the hall was not of the sports variety but a function room laid out for a banquet and clustered with chandeliers. It may not surprise some readers that both players came from the west of Offa's Dyke.

The idea of moving the ball off the pitch may seem extreme or even fatuous and I admit that there is little likelihood that defence coaches will spend much of their time teaching their charges how to read the wrong'un from a leg break, but I am sure that the variety and extent of kicks available (with both foot and knee) have not been thoroughly explored. We already have the kick to the wing standing wide. So why not to the outside centre cutting the angle? Perhaps the cross kick is due a reappearance. The cautious will worry about losing possession but a player takes that risk every time he passes the ball. At the very least, it would make the defence consider another option that it has to cover and so be forced to stretch its resources to the advantage of the attacker. The game is, after all, still called Rugby Football.

Another area that coaches might consider is the number of scores that occur after the ball has accidentally hit the ground during the course of a passage of play. It seems to fix a defence in the way that a dummy runner rarely does. It may be that the thought of a turn-over produces a rush of blood and the defender ignores his zonal duties in the hope of gaining possession but, more likely, the unexpected or unusual causes a moment of indecision or a lack of concentration as to the whereabouts of the attacking players. I am not suggesting Aussie Rules dribbling or the basketball V pass but the occasional introduction of something entirely unexpected, where the opposition is lured into ball-watching rather than defending, might produce interesting results.

The second area of doubt is whether or not the game can stand on its own two fiscal feet. The bottom line is that a professional club must generate sufficient money to pay its staff. The only way that this can be assured is an agreed salary cap among the clubs concerned to control the wages and security of tenure in the Premiership to ensure the income. Both these propositions have their opponents. The better supported clubs would claim they are entitled to spend their own money as they want and those in the lower divisions would argue that the whole point of a league system is that it must allow promotion and relegation. As usual, both sides have a point. As one owner of a Premier Club pointed out, if you leased a property you would never consider effecting any improvements if you knew you could be kicked out at the end of twelve months. Perhaps the attached garden is a more appropriate metaphor than the flat: you might plant the odd annual or two but would never contemplate investing in beds of perennials, the flowering of which you may never see. And to make matters worse, petunias, particularly those of a southern hemisphere strain, don't come cheap.

A compromise might be to make relegation and promotion between the Premier League and the First Division a biennial or triennial event. The bottom team of the Premier League would be that which had the lowest cumulative number of points over the period in question and the top two of the First Division the greatest. A play-off would produce one winner who would be a member of the Premier League for the following seasons. The simple advantage of this would be to stop the yo-yo effect that is likely to occur because a newly promoted club does not have time to find its feet (as would have happened to Leeds) and give Premiership Clubs and serious contenders for that league an incentive to build their playing strength on a settled base rather than buying their way out of trouble or into glory. The last thing the English game at any level needs is to have its Premier League peopled by players who are not eligible for the national side.

The likelihood of this happening appears to have increased as a result of a recent ruling by the European Court of Justice. Moras Kolpak, a Slovakian handball player, took the German Handball Federation to court, claiming that the quota system preventing clubs employing more than two non-EU nationals was illegal. The court found in his favour, deciding that such a system discriminated against countries who had an association or co-operative agreement with the EU. South Africa and the South Sea Islands number among such countries. Prima facie, this would put an end to the quota system currently in place in English rugby (one non-EU player for domestic matches, two for European competitions) and allow clubs, possibly at the expense of their youth development, to buy overseas players to support their championship bid or stave off relegation.

Although there is evidence to support the latter, it is unlikely that a club would disrupt a side that was going well. The mercenary will probably move on and the disgruntled players who have been dropped to accommodate the next messiah may well have done likewise. Moreover, there is a caveat to these *Jeux Sans Frontiers.* The player in question has to have a work permit and the qualification for such in the UK is that he must have played in 75% of his country's international matches over the previous two years. So the field is pretty limited. If the players in question are current Internationals, they are unlikely to jeopardise their chances of future selection by moving to England. If not, they have probably lost the edge both physically and mentally and will want to play a game that hides their diminishing powers. Not a good basis for a club building for the future. In any event, no one could afford, in the manner of soccer, to buy a team of stars. There is just not enough money in club rugby. International rugby is a different matter. What might be more worrying would be if a gang of Antipodeans claimed EU citizenship on the back of their parents' passports and started playing for Italy.

More immediately pressing is that the whole business of leagues has had a serious effect on the English game at large. Virtually every club in the country is involved in one league or another. Human nature being what it is, the success or otherwise of a club is measured by its relative position to other clubs in the area—not only by the club members but by would-be players and potential sponsors. An aspiring club's First team squad, to comply with safety requirements and to cover injury or rest key members, will require a minimum of 25 players, its second team twenty players. Suddenly, simple arithmetic tells you that the Third XV has disappeared. Clubs that once ran six sides now run half that number. Playing membership dwindles and, with it, the attached income. The First team may be promoted and the club faces greater expense as travelling and other costs increase. Conversely, relegation is often the start of a rapid downward spiral and clubs that once would have regarded themselves as among the best in their region, if not in the land, find themselves among the also-rans. Eventually, expenditure outweighs both income and enthusiasm and club after club folds.

This is the Doomsday scenario that the RFU faces as it runs its Community Programme. If the membership of clubs declines and the number of clubs becomes less, then the platform of its playing and financial structure becomes very wobbly. The whole strategy it has devised is based on volunteers who as ex-players beaver away at the weekend and cough up their forty odd quid a go to attend Twickenham six times a season. If the source were to dry up or even be significantly reduced, then the alarm bells would be ringing in no uncertain manner. There is also some doubt as to what they can do about it. The simplest answer would be to regulate the game as if it were a commercial concern. Two clubs in the same area: each can run one and a half teams and neither has sufficient income to cover expenditure. Solution: combine the two and sell the more profitable piece of real estate to Tesco. Result: one club, three teams, double the income to cover the same expenditure and money in the bank to develop the facilities and put into place proper coaching and development plans. But local rivalry dies hard and before the arguments have disappeared as to which colour should predominate on the combined strip, many players and key workers fed up with the wrangling might well have slipped away. Result: another club with one and a half teams and insufficient income to cover expenditure. The RFU could insist. Make it a condition of membership of the Union that certain standards are met, that clubs run a certain number of teams. But it would be a dangerous road to travel and could well destroy the grass roots they depend on. I wonder, when they (whoever 'they' were) pronounced the game open, how many of them considered the exact wormy nature of the can they were opening. Perhaps they thought–again, like Macbeth–'If it were done, when 'tis done, then 'twere well/It were done quickly.' And we all know what happened to him.

9

The Shape of Things to Come

Although I am writing this some months before the 2003 World Cup, the book will probably reach the shops after the Final is done and dusted. So, in this version of back to the future, any assessment is a guess rather than a post-mortem. All I know before going to print is that England are unbeaten, but not unbeatable, and New Zealand seem to be thumping everyone south of the Tropic of Capricorn. However, it would not take a clairvoyant to prophesy that the semi-finalists will be Australia, England, France and New Zealand or, put it this way, you won't find a bookie who will give you decent odds against it.

There could be upsets. Australia have an awkward group, with an opening match against Argentina and a possible group decider against Ireland, but the odds of the hosts going out early are slim. The occasion might make South Africa rise from the ashes and the French might move into sulk mode, but I suspect the real interest in the early games is whether the emerging nations can replace the long-established home unions in the pecking order. The bookies' final is New Zealand *v* England. Over a series of matches you would fancy New Zealand nous coupled with explosive South Seas pace to prevail. But, in a one-off, this young and relatively inexperienced side might not have sufficient poise to beat a team that knows that its best and, for some, last chance to lift the trophy is on Saturday 22nd November 2003.

What is more interesting is to look for the unexpected. Which particular elements of the good, the bad and the ugly will surface this time round? I hope, for the game at large, that there are moments of innovation and individual brilliance that catch the attention of the uncommitted public and inspire the young. For obvious reasons, the various countries have been keeping their aces up their sleeves as no team escapes the presence of the omnipresent video camera. Each coach will have his own plans but I am particularly interested in how England are going to use Jason Robinson. As a decoy runner he must open spaces for others, but I suspect his role will be greater than that. However, it is not clear what his best options are and in this lies a strength. If England have yet to decide, it is very difficult–unlike, for example, with Jonah Lomu–for the opposition to develop a counter-plan. All that can be said at the moment is that it is clear that he is not the Rugby Union archetypal full back who arrives late and at speed into the line, and attempts to play him in this role have not been particularly successful.

Like Healy before him, Robinson seems to have a free-roaming role, turning up at the moment when he can cause the most damage, but even this does not seem to work as well as it could. It might pay Woodward and his advisers to have another look at the cross-codes games played between Wigan and Bath, at the time regarded as the best in each version of the game. It was particularly when the match was played under League rules that Robinson was at his most effective. Not surprisingly, you might think. But the modern Union defence system is not unlike League and therefore might be broken in the same way. In the League game, the Bath 13 dutifully lined up across the field, secure in the knowledge that if the leaguers kicked, the unionists would regain possession. The ball went to Robinson on the wing, at which point he strolled across the face of Bath's defensive line as if inspecting the troops. The Union players were not certain what to do. If they dived in, he would beat them on the spot, if they held the line he would wait until he came across a gap sufficiently wide to scamper through. There was no need for a dummy; the dummies had sold themselves. In other words, his essential skill is moving laterally at speed whilst having the perfect balance to move forward instantaneously and even quicker. When he runs from the back, it is relatively easy for a defence to set up a gang of three to cover all manoeuvres. When it has less time, it might be more difficult. If it could be arranged for him to be first receiver at various critical moments, the results might be interesting.

One possibility is to play him at scrum half at the breakdown, not in the orthodox sense of putting the ball in, etc, but to create the one-on-one opportunity that he can so easily exploit, particularly if, for a moment or two, seven are playing against seven. It is clear that a number of coaches feel, as League did so many years ago, that the best chance of scoring, or at least of exciting play, is when the donkeys are communally grazing in a restricted part of the field. And it is in this area that the bad, or so some might think, could take place. There is no doubt that there is going to be a good deal of blocking by players running not with intention of catching the ball but deliberately to cross the defence's flight path at a critical moment. Some of this may be within the laws but other moments will not and I suspect that the illegal variations will come after a set piece. If you take one man out of seven, the defence becomes immediately very vulnerable. An interesting example of this would be an attacking lineout thirty yards out. Split two-man called, with ball off the top and in possession of the first receiver at maximum speed. If he cuts back into the 25-yard wide space that is available to him, he will face, at the most, four defenders. If two of these are taken out as the result of judicial placing of the body by his team mates and the first receiver is strong, powerful and elusive, you would fancy his chances against whatever opposition remained. If he broke through, there would be nothing between him and the line. The aim of all coaches will be to pit their best players against the weakest point of the opposition's defence and one way to create weakness is to take key players out of the game. It is not that difficult. I recall a referee from a highly respected school in the north of England who always stood at the tail of the line when his team threw in and at the front when it was the opposition's turn. It may be that he felt that he had a better view that way and that it was just unfortunate that the away team's fly half had to circumnavigate a by now retreating and not insubstantial figure before he could make a tackle. As I have said, it is not necessarily bad. There is nothing inherently wrong with blocking. After all, the Americans have been doing it for years.

The ugly is usually associated with tabloid calumny, body-enhancing drugs, food poisoning and the like, and there is one scandal that may well emerge. That is industrial espionage. As Rugby Union is an artificial game, there are a number of moments when it stops completely. In such a hiatus there is an opportunity for a team to agree on some prearranged plan of action. The most obvious of these is the lineout where an agreed code links thrower to catcher. It would be an enormous advantage to the defending side if it was also in the know. The normal method is a series of lineout calls which indicates the flight of the throw and the person who is to catch it. It has always been acceptable for the opposition to try to crack the code on the field and this often happens. The stance of the hooker or the position of his arm, immediately before the throw-in takes place, can give the game away and studying videos of past games is commonplace. But what if it is taken further?

Hidden microphones at the training ground, mysterious disappearances of the coach's clipboard or, worse, the beans being spilt by disaffected or unscrupulous squad members. It is not too fanciful. Dodgy betting and dishonest practice have pervaded other sports and there is no reason to assume that the creaking armour of amateurism will be able to resist the sinister lance of professional blandishment.

As I have said, all this will have been resolved before these pages are turned. So, enough of mediaeval panoply and let's take a stab at the future. What will the form book say about the sides that qualify for the World Cup in 2007? I have already said enough about England. They have a large player base, an ethnic mix that ensures a variety of athletic attributes, an untapped reservoir of talent that is currently attracted to Rugby League, a sound financial base and an enthusiastic group of supporters. You would have to try quite hard to make a mess of that. In the same way, Australia and New Zealand will always be in the frame in the foreseeable future. They not only have the talent and enthusiasm but also the mindset— the former that they should be the best at every sport they go in for, the latter because it is part of the national heritage. Until these attitudes change, that

197

relatively underpopulated part of the world will punch considerably more than its weight. What is more, they seem to be doing their own fair share of ethnic mixing by adding the flair, power and pace of the South Pacific to their already formidable resources.

As a consequence of this, the likes of Samoa and other islands will have their natural talent drained away and become less and less likely to have an impact on the competition. Professionalism may well prove a double-edged sword to these peoples. The Celts might also suffer in the same way. The change in the economic structure in Britain has meant people have had to move to find work. As a result, the offspring may well not be born in the land of their fathers. If playing for and in England is both more lucrative and convenient than playing for the home country, many with dual qualification may choose the profitable rather than historical alternative. The Irish will probably be less affected. They have a sound structure based on the provinces and the country, at the moment, is in good economic shape. It also has its own player reservoir. It would be interesting to know how many League players are eligible for the old country. In fact the Irish, with their history of mass emigration, could spread the net far and wide if they so wished.

The Americas, with their racial mix, should have the ability to produce outstanding sides, but the northern part of the continent is, in sporting terms, very much inward-looking, seeing only its own home-grown team games to be of any real importance, and the likes of soccer and particularly rugby are left to the ex-pats. As for South America, rugby, when it is played, is very much an upper class game and, in a continent where the way out of the gutter is to emulate Pele and Maradona, there is little likelihood that soccer will lose its grip. Also, in the areas where interest is shown, the indigenous population is often, like Japan, too small in stature. There is no doubt that the Japanese tried every way to overcome this handicap and it is extremely unlikely that others will prevail where they have failed.

In southern Europe, rugby players come from a narrow social band and until they broaden that base, countries such as Italy, Spain and Portugal probably won't compete at a serious level. There are patches, like Rumania, in the rest of Europe but poor economic conditions mean that the game will only flourish sporadically. The exception to this is the French. Potentially, they are always the most dangerous rugby-playing nation, capable of beating anyone, anywhere. If, now that the game has gone officially professional, they were to absorb the better elements of other rugby cultures, they might add consistency to their undoubted talents.

This leaves the enigma of South Africa. Before the rugby fraternity decided to exercise its own form of apartheid, it was arguably the strongest rugby nation in the world and would have been an automatic favourite for any World Cup. Even the All Blacks gave little for their chances once they entered the high veldt. Now one wonders if they will ever find themselves in that position again. Once more, it is a matter of mindset. The existence of racial discrimination is based on the assumption that one race is inherently superior to another. The South Africans must have believed that their European stock was of a higher order than the native African, and rugby selection and attitude have been, and necessarily must still be, influenced by this way of thinking. As time has proved, the European countries that were best at empire-building might also have been the best at inventing athletic team games, but that does not mean they are necessarily the best at playing them.